SEXUAL HARASSMENT IN THE POST OFFICE

FRANCIS DI CANDIO

Sexual Harassment in the Post Office

This book is written to provide information and motivation to readers. Its purpose is not to render any type of psychological, legal, or professional advice of any kind. The content is the sole opinion and expression of the author, and not necessarily that of the publisher.

Copyright © 2021 by Francis Di Candio.

All rights reserved. No part of this book may be reproduced, transmitted, or distributed in any form by any means, including, but not limited to, recording, photocopying, or taking screenshots of parts of the book, without prior written permission from the author or the publisher. Brief quotations for noncommercial purposes, such as book reviews, permitted by Fair Use of the U.S. Copyright Law, are allowed without written permissions, as long as such quotations do not cause damage to the book's commercial value. For permissions, write to the publisher, whose address is stated below.

Printed in the United States of America.

ISBN 978-1-953150-86-8   (Paperback)
ISBN 978-1-955363-71-6   (Hardback)
ISBN 978-1-953150-87-5   (Digital)

Lettra Press books may be ordered through booksellers or by contacting:

Lettra Press LLC
30 N Gould St. Suite 4753
Sheridan, WY 82801
1 307-200-3414 | info@lettrapress.com
www.lettrapress.com

Dedication

I dedicate this book to my doctor and staff, for putting all my medical documentation together, and for being so kind and patient.

I want to thank my psychiatrist, for getting me through my mental anxiety from dealing with the postal service.

My special thanks to the congressman, for helping me through his correspondence with the post office, and for helping me with my sexual harassment.

I want to thank my friend Kathy (not her real name) for being there when I needed her.

I would like to thank my husband, "Don Goodfellow," who supports me and encourages me to go forward.

How can I forget my friend Benny (not his real name), for helping me put this book in order, and for giving me support and believing in me.

ACKNOWLEDGEMENTS

I would like to acknowledge the following people for assisting me in the creation of this book:

I want to thank the president of the Local-2, and the shop stewards, for trying to help me with this case.

Thanks to the president of Local-3, for winning the COD case and for helping me along the way.

Special thanks to the Local-1 president and our shop steward for giving me support and being there when I needed them the most.

Thanks to all of the wonderful, giving friends. Thanks for your support letters.

Thanks to all my friends who, over the years, have shared their love and support.

Thanks to God, that I didn't become postal in a violent way.

I WAS BORN JUNE TWENTIETH, ON FATHER'S DAY, in a small town in Puerto Rico. I come from a very poor family. My mother had five children, all girls, named Carmela, Emily, myself, Patricia, and Aidita, who died from diarrhea and vomiting. My mother was a great cook, and friendly with everyone. My mother raised me with the truth.

My father spent time in the armed services. The first time I saw him, I was four or five years old. That afternoon, my mother sent me to get my sisters from around the corner, and when I came out of the house, a car was parked two houses down from mine. A man opened the door of the car and called to me. I told the man that my mother had told me not to talk to strangers, but a woman called me by my name, Amira. I recognized the woman. It was Susie, my uncle's ex-wife, and I went to the car.

The man put me on his lap and kissed me on my left cheek, and he asked me, "Where is your father?" I told him that my father was fixing the stairs for Zulma (my stepfather). His eyes got watery, and he gave me a white box and told me to share the cookies with my sisters. He kissed me again, and they left.

I ran to my mother, who was in the house, and I told her a man gave me a box of cookies. She asked me, "What man?" And I told her he was a man with four eyes (meaning he was wearing glasses). My mother pointed to a picture that was on the wall and asked me, "That man?" And I told her, "Yes, that man, Mommy."

My mother ran to the balcony, and I followed her. With a smile on her face, she started to look all around, and I asked her, "Who was that man?" She told me, "That man is your father." That was the first and last time I saw my father.

My mother and stepfather moved to a new place. I had a nice childhood, living there. My stepfather, who was a carpenter, worked hard to give us everything that we needed. I loved him a lot. When he was working, and it was time for lunch, I was the one who took the food to him, helped him with the cement, and put the tiles in the bathroom where he was working. My stepfather showed me how, even though I was a little girl. But after years of my mother being with my stepfather, they broke up. I never knew the reason why they went their separate ways.

When I was twelve years old, I met a guy named Tito, who was sixteen years old. After months of being with him, Tito took my virginity. When I got home, I took a shower, put my pajamas on, and went to bed.

Early in the morning, when I woke up, I went to my best friend Rachael's house, and I told her what Tito had done to me. She got really angry and said to me, "Let's go." And she took me back home, and told my mother that Tito had taken my virginity. My mother took me to the police precinct and made a report. The police officer asked my mother what she wanted to do, and my mother told him that she wanted Tito to pay for what he had done to me.

The police officers went to Tito's house, at the caserio, and they took him to the precinct. Tito saw me sitting there with my mother, and he said to me, "Hi, Amiraton," and I said hi to him. The police officer took him to a room to ask him questions, and when the officer finished, he called my mother and me into the room. The officer told my mother that Tito was going to marry me. My mother didn't like Tito. She had told me that he was a bad kid. But I was "in love," and didn't listen to my mother, and Tito took me to live with him at his grandmother's apartment en el caserio.

Then I got pregnant. I was fifteen years old, and we were still living at his grandmother's house; in the house, there was no electricity and no gas. I had to light candles. I would cook on the patio, where would I put three big rocks; with wood in the middle of the rocks, that was my stove. I lived there for nine months.

Early one morning, I woke up with severe pain, and Tito took me to the hospital a couple of blocks from the house. The ambulance took me to Ponce, where I had my son. I named him Rickuel.

I stayed in the hospital for three days, and when I came out, I went to live with my mother. When my mother saw me, she said to me, "Do you want to be a mother? I will show you how to become a good mother."

When my son started crying, my mother never ran to him. She told me, "Your son is crying, see what's wrong with him." One day, my son started crying, nonstop, and my mother told me what to do: "Give him milk." But the baby didn't want milk. She said, "Change the diaper." I did, but the diaper was not wet. She said, "Get the gas out of him." I put my son against my chest and started to hit his back gently to get his gas out, but my son kept on crying. My mother took my son from my hands and walked to the kitchen. I went into the kitchen, too. She put a pot with a little bit of oil on the stove and asked me for a gotero, an ear dropper. She put the warm oil in the gotero and put one drop in each of my son's ears. She held her grandson, and put him to sleep.

What my son had was an ear infection. My mother looked at me, and I told her, "I love you a lot."

I took my son everywhere I went. The one that babysat for me was my little sister, Patricia, and only when I was going to see Tito. My mother did the best she could to take care of my son with milk, baby food, diapers, and clothes.

One day, Tito told me that he was going to New York, and he would send for me as soon as possible.

I would come to the United States.

In December, Tito sent me an airplane ticket to go to New York. In January, I came to the United States. I was fifteen years old, and my son was going to be one year old in a couple of days.

When I arrived at the airport, I was lost. I could not find Tito. A man saw me looking around the airport, and he asked me if someone was coming to pick me up. l told him that my baby's father hadn't come to get me. The man said, "I will help you look for your baby's father." He said, "By the way, my name is Tony," and I said my name was Amira. And he told me, "Come with me, I am going to talk to the receptionist," and I followed him.

When we got to the desk, he told the receptionist to page my boyfriend, Tito. The receptionist paged him, but he never answered. It was early morning, and it was really cold. Tony asked me what part of New York I was going to, and I showed him the address. He told me, "Don't worry, you will not stay here," and he started to ask people for a ride; but no one would help us. Then we walked through the airport, and he asked a man who was with his family. Tony said we needed a ride home, and lied to the man, saying that I was his wife. The man with his family took us to Tony's address. Tony thanked the man for driving us, saying that it was very nice of him. And we went inside the building. I think it was in the Bronx.

Tony opened the door, and we went inside the apartment. He told me to get comfortable. I started to look around the three-bedroom apartment. And he told me, "You are going to sleep in that room." Inside the room was a bedroom set and a crib. Tony told me that my son could sleep in the crib, and I could sleep on the bed. I asked him, "And where are you going to sleep?" And he said, "I am going to sleep in the living room." I said goodnight to him, and I closed the door to the room. I put my baby in the crib and went to sleep.

After I fell asleep, Tony called to me: "Hey, hey." I opened my eyes, and he was sitting on the edge of the bed. He told me that he wanted to have sex with me, and he asked if I wanted to do it with him. I told him that I was going to see my baby's father, and he said, "Okay, sorry." Tony left the room, and I stood up from the bed, really fast. I closed the door and put a chair under the doorknob.

In the morning, when I woke up, Tony wasn't in the apartment. I said in to myself, *Oh my gosh, what I am going to do now?* I went to the bathroom and washed my face, and I heard someone opening the door. I got really nervous, but when the door opened, I saw that it was Tony, with a bag in his hand. I was really happy to see him because I thought that he had left me there by myself.

He told me that he had gone downstairs to get breakfast, and when he finished eating, he was going to take me to Brooklyn. I told him, "Okay, gracias, thank you." We ate breakfast, and I gave my son his bottle. When he finished drinking his milk, I dressed him, we went downstairs, and Tony's friend was waiting for us in front of the building. Tony introduced me to him. We walked to the train station, and I took the train for the first time. There were so many people; I held my baby real tight.

Tony took me to the address that I gave him, we went inside the building, and he knocked on the first-floor door to the right. A woman answered the door, and Tony told her that I was looking for Tito, and she told Tony that Tito wasn't there, to look for him at the bodega around the corner of Wilson and Woodbine.

Tony took me to the bodega, and Tito was there. When Tito saw me, he got really happy and grabbed the baby and started to kiss him. Tony told Tito that I was lost at the airport, and Tito told me that he had gone to the airport to get me, but I never arrived, and he left, because he thought that I wasn't coming to New York. Tito thanked Tony for helping me, and Tony and his friend talked to Tito for a while, and then they left.

Tito took me inside a building on the same block, and he opened the door of the first-floor apartment, but when I went inside, it was empty. I asked Tito where the bed was. He told me, "For tonight, we will sleep on the floor."

The three of us slept on the floor that night, but the next day, in the afternoon, Tito came in with a box spring, four crates to place the box spring on top of, and a playpen for the baby.

Tito was working at the bodega for the owner of the building, Pancho, so we could stay in the apartment. After a month of staying in the apartment, a woman named Yvette took me to the welfare center. I tried to get public assistance, but the worker told me that I was too young to get it, and I left the center.

One day, Tito came to the apartment and told me that we had to move to the next building because Pancho had rented the apartment. I asked Tito, "What are we going to do?" Tito told me that Pancho was the owner of the building. We went to live in a four-room apartment on the third floor. Even after being in the United States for a couple of months, it was still hard, because I could not buy the things that I needed for my son and myself. Tito decided to apply for public assistance, to see if he could open the case using his name. After a couple of months, they opened a case for us. The caseworker gave us an emergency allowance and money to buy furniture.

I bought a bed and a kitchen table. Tito's friend gave us a nice living room set and a crib for my son, Rick.

RAPE

I got pregnant again, and I had my second son. I named him John. When Rick was a year and eight months, we moved to a four-bedroom1 apartment in Brooklyn, on the Lop floor.

One night, Tito went out, and I stayed home, watching television and taking care of my two sons. I put my older son, Rick, in his' room to sleep, and after I finished watching television, I went to sleep. My younger son John, was sleeping on the bed with me, because I didn't have a crib for him.

At about three o'clock in the morning, Rick woke up for his bottle. I went to the kitchen and prepared his bottle of milk, and when I went back to the room and turned on the lights, I noticed the curtains from the window were on the floor. I gave 1ny son the bottle, and he finished drinking his milk. I went to the kitchen to get a hammer and some nails, and started nailing the curtains back on the window frame.

I asked myself how the curtains came off the window frame, but when I finished nailing the curtains, l went back to sleep.

A noise woke me up, and when I opened my eyes, I saw a man standing next to my bed; he had a bandana covering his face. When I tried to scream, the man covered my mouth with his left hand and told me, "Don't scream, or I will kill your baby." He had a big knife in his right hand. I thought I was going to die when he told me those words.

I just moved my head, saying *yes*, and started crying and crying. I was terrified for my son. I told the man to take the money, the stereo, and the television. The man told me, "What I want is you."

I sat down slowly on the bed and started feeling under the mattress, looking for the machete that Tito always kept there, but I could not find it. I stood up really slowly from the bed, and the man put me against the wall. I cried and cried, begging him not to hurt me, and he told me, "If you don't do it, I will kill your baby." And he raped me.

When he finished raping me, I heard a noise coming from the kitchen. It was my puppy, who was in the bathroom. I told the man to leave because my husband was coming home. But the man, with the knife in his hand, walked to the kitchen to see who was coming.

I cried and cried, nonstop. I wanted to leave out the window, but I couldn't, because I had my older son in the other room, sleeping. The man came back to the room and left through the window.

I looked all around the room. I could not think, I was so terrified, and I ran from my apartment and started to knock on my friends' door. I knocked and knocked, terrified that the man was going to come and get me again. My friend's brother-in-law opened the door, and I started to cry while he asked me, "Amira, what happened?"

I could not answer him. I was in shock. He asked me, "Something happen to the kids?" And the only thing that I could do was cry. He had to slap me on my face twice, and then I told him that a man had raped me.

He ran to his room and got a machete. He woke up his brother, and they ran to my apartment. My other two friends woke up and went to my apartment, and got my two sons. The only thing that I saw in my mind was the man raping me. My friend's husband ran to the roof, but they could not find the man who had raped me.

I stayed at my friends' apartment until Tito came home at about 4:30 in the morning. Tito knocked on my friend's door, and when I saw him, I started to cry. He asked me, "What happened?" My friend told him, "She got raped, where were you?" Tito said to me, "Let's go home."

We went to my apartment, which was on the same floor, and I went to the bathroom and got into the shower with my clothes on. I was crying, and Tito came into the shower with me and asked, "It is true?" And I told him, "He was going to kill my baby."

I was in shock for a couple of months, and it took more than a year for me to recover. I moved from there to New York Avenue in Brooklyn, but I was very sad in that apartment, because I was far away from my sister and friends.

A couple of months later, I moved to Wilson Avenue in Brooklyn, to a four-room apartment. I moved after the first blackout that we had in New York. At Wilson Avenue, I was really happy. I had my friends, Joan and Isabel, and a lady named Flora.

They were like my family. They helped me a lot. Isabel's daughter Elisabeth was taking Rick, who was four years old, and John, who was years old, to church. The church had activities for the children, and every summer they took Rick to camp, but John was too small to go with them. He started going to camp went he was four years old.

Rick started school in September, and it was the happiest time for me, taking my son to school for the first time. He was a very smart kid, and very alert. Rick started kindergarten two years later; he was a real quiet kid, but very smart. The same year, Tito went to jail. It was the worst thing for me, having my kids' father in jail, but I went to see him every week.

One afternoon, I was in my apartment with my friend Madeline, and someone knocked on the door. When I looked through the peephole, I saw that it was my sister Emily. I opened the door, and I said to her, "What a miracle it is to see you! Come in." And she looked at me, really sad. I asked her, "What is wrong?" She told me that our mother was in the hospital in a coma, and Madeline said, "I am sorry to hear that."

I walked to the sofa, sat down, and started crying. Emily told· me that Mommy was at the hospital in Ponce, and my other sister Carmela, who was in Puerto Rico, was going to call. her to give her more information.

When Emily left, I went upstairs and asked my friend Aurora to watch my kids, and I told her about my dearest mother. She said, "Don't worry, I will watch your kids," and I went to my aunt's house, on Woodbine Avenue and Bushwick Avenue, and I told her that I didn't have any money to go and see my mother. She gave me the money to buy a plane ticket, and I said to her, "Aunt Sica, thank you very much," and she said, "Go and buy the ticket as soon as possible," and I left her house.

I went back to Aurora's apartment, and I asked her if she could lend me some money, and she gave me the money to buy the return ticket. She told me, "Don't you worry about the kids. My daughter will take care of them." I told her, "Thank you for everything that you are doing for me." The next day, Madeline came home with an envelope and told me that she had done a collection for me. She gave me the envelope, and when I opened it, I found $200 dollars inside.

I told her "Thank you," and I called my sister Emily to tell her that I was going to buy the plane tickets. She told me to wait until she could get her money together. I did wait for her, and my mother died the second my sister got her airplane ticket.

My mother died at fifty-two years old.

My sister and I left for Puerto Rico, and when we got there my mother was at the funeral home.

I did all nine rosaries and stayed in Puerto Rico for almost a month, cleaning my mother's apartment before flying back to New York.

One day, the landlord sold the building, and the new owner raised the rent. I couldn't afford to pay the new rent, and he took me to court.

While at court, I was looking for another apartment. I met a woman, and I told her about my problem, and she told me that she had an apartment in her single-family house. She gave me her telephone number.

After I finished at court, I went home and called the woman to make an appointment. She gave me an appointment for the next afternoon.

Went I got there, she showed me the apartment, three box rooms and a bathroom, but no kitchen. I liked it, even if it had no kitchen. I said to myself, *I can manage this.*

And I moved into the apartment, in 1984. I went to the welfare center and told my caseworker that I had found an apartment for less money, and she said "Okay", and she did the paperwork. I found a side job cleaning a house to pay the extra rent.

My kids' father came home from jail and started using drugs. He started taking everything from the apartment and selling it. One evening, I came home from work, and my two sons were crying. I asked them what was wrong, and Rick told me that his father had taken his book bag, his sneakers, his jacket, and his hat. I told them, "Don't cry, Mommy will buy you more."

Tito came home at about eleven o'clock that night, and he woke me up. I asked him why he did that to his own children, but he could not answer me. He just went to the bathroom, came out, and went outside.

I was crying because of what he was doing in my bathroom: drugs. I told Tito to please leave, because I was going to leave him, but he laughed at me. I cried the whole night through.

In the morning, I prepared the kids for school. The kids left, and it was time for me to go to work. Tito told me, "You are not going anywhere." My eyes were red, because I had been crying all night, and he said to me, "You are coming with me."

He took me to a place in Brooklyn. I stood next to a parked car, while I watched him sell pills for his habit. I was saying, in my mind, I am going to leave him tonight; I can take no more.

While looking at Tito, I saw a car parking behind the car that I was standing next to. Three tall white men jumped out of the car. They grabbed Tito and pushed him against the wall, searched him, handcuffed him, and put him in the car.

When I saw the detectives take Tito away, I started laughing and crying at the same time, because God knew that I was going to do something crazy that night.

Something was telling me, "My keys." I went to the car and told one of the detectives, "My keys, I got to get my kids at school." The detective asked me, "What?" I told him he had my keys, and I had to get my kids at school. The detective looked at me, I looked at him, and he got my keys from Tito's pants pocket.

I told the detective "Thank you,", and I left. I went to visit Tito in jail at the correctional facility in New York. When he saw me, he came over to the table, and he was going to kiss me. I told him, "I didn't come here for kisses; I came here because I was going to leave my home without a place to go with my kids."

What he did was laugh at me. I stood up from the chair, and I said to him, "keep on laughing," and I left the visiting room, thinking that I never wanted to see him again.

One evening, I came home from work, and I found everything from the living room moved to the kids' room. I called the cops. When the cops came to my apartment, I showed them what had happened. The cop asked me who was living in the house, and I told them that the only people living in the house were a married couple downstairs, and me, with my kids; no one else.

They went downstairs to talk to the couple about what had happened in my apartment. The man and his wife acted like they didn't know anything. I asked the man, "How could you do something like that to my kids and me?" They didn't answer me, but deep in my heart I knew it was them. I moved from that apartment to try to forget about my past, especially my son's father.

I moved to Queens. I rented a big one-family house, just for my kids and myself. I was very happy there with my children for about one year and a couple of months, but Rick missed his friends. He wasn't happy.

One day, the landlady came home to tell me that she was going to sell the house, and I had to move. I got very sad, so I moved back to Brooklyn, and lost my job.

One night, I took a walk, and a woman I knew saw me, and she called me over and introduced me to her friend Don, an Italian man, and asked if I wanted to go with them to the Island. I told her, "Okay."

After living on that street for a year, the landlady raised the rent, and I could not pay the extra because I didn't have a job. The landlady took me to tenants' and landlords' court, and we made an agreement for me to get the money within a short period of time.

I could not get the money in time, so I went back to court, and the judge gave me more time. A Dominican man, a good friend of mine, gave me the money to pay the rent, and I went to the real estate office and gave the rent money to the woman who was coming to collect the rent every month. She gave me a receipt, and I left the office.

One night, I came home to my apartment and could not open the door. I tried and tried, and nothing happened. When I looked, there was a paper on the door. I took it off the door, and it was from the marshal. I asked myself, *What is going on?*

Then I went downstairs to Carmen's apartment on the second floor, and knocked on the door. When she opened it, I asked her, "Can you believe that the marshal locked me out?" She told me to come in and relax. I told her that I paid the rent, and that my receipt was in the apartment. I waited for my sons at Carmen's apartment.

My younger son knocked on the door, because he had heard me talking from the hallway. He was with his friend, Tommy; I looked at him and told him that we could not stay in the apartment. He asked me, "Why?" I told him the reason. Tommy told me not to worry about Rick; that he was going to take him to his house to sleep, and I told him, "This is something serious, what's your mother going to say?" He told me not to worry, and that he was going to talk to his mother. Rick asked me, "Mommy, what are you going to do?" And I told him, "I will be fine, tomorrow I will go to court."

Tommy took Rick to his mother's apartment in the projects. Rick came home after John, and I told him that we had lost the apartment; he asked me, "What do you mean, we lost the apartment?" I told him that the marshal had locked us out, and he had to stay in one of his friend's houses. He told me that he was going to stay at his girlfriend's house. I told him, "Okay," and he left.

That night, I stayed at one of my friend's apartments. The next day, I went to court, but I could not see the judge. They gave me an appointment date. Waiting for the appointment, I went back to Carmen's apartment, and I said to her, "I need to go inside the apartment and look for my important papers and the rent receipt."

I was really scared to do something like that, because that was trespassing, and I could go to jail. Carmen said to me, "Let's go and see if the super is downstairs. We went downstairs and she knocked a couple of times on the basement door, where the super was living, but he wasn't there. I told Carmen that my appointment in court was in two days, and I was going to tell the judge what they had done to me. She told me that she was going to try again later or the next day, to see if the super had the keys.

I left, and the super didn't let me in, but I went to see the judge, and I told him that the marshal had locked me out. I said I had gone to the real estate office and gave the rent money to the woman who went to the building to collect the rent every month. I cried to the judge, and the judge told me that I could go back to my apartment, and that if the door wasn't open, I should break it. I told the judge, "No, thanks. That woman tore my family apart."

I left the courtroom, and I never went back to the apartment. I left everything behind. I stayed at different places until I spoke to a woman named Gloria, and she spoke to her husband, named Octavio, arid they let me stay with them. It was really nice of Gloria to let me stay in her apartment with her family of six. She didn't know me that well.

Don took me out for the first time.

One afternoon, I told Lynda, Gloria's older daughter, to walk with me to the restaurant to get wonton soup, because my stomach wasn't feeling well. While I was walking with Lynda, I heard a horn, and when I looked I saw a red Suzuki. It was Don, the man that the woman had introduced me to. Don called me over, and I went to see what he wanted.

Don said hello, and he asked me how I was doing. I told him, "Fine." He looked at me and wrote his telephone number on a heart card from Las Vegas, and he told me to call him. I just looked at him and said, "Okay, bye."

Then I left to go to the restaurant to get my wonton soup. When I went back to Gloria's apartment, I told Gloria that Don, an Italian man, had given me his number to call him, and Gloria said to me, "Well, call him." I told Gloria that the only thing he wanted was a piece of me. Gloria told me that I didn't have anything to lose, and for me to call him.

So, I did call Don, and I asked him why he gave me his number. He told me that he wanted to take me to dinner or to Fortunado for cappuccino. I told him okay.

That night, he came to get me, and we decided to go to a cafe in Brooklyn, because I had already eaten before he picked me up. When we got there, we got a table, and when the waitress came, he asked for a cappuccino and a lulu, and I asked for the same. When I took a sip of the coffee, I told Don that it was the first time I had drunk cappuccino, and it was delicious. We stayed there, talking for a while, and then Don took me home.

While Don was driving, he tried to touch my leg with his right hand. I hit his hand and I told him, "Please, no," and he didn't try to touch me again. When we were in front of the building, he gave me a kiss on my cheek, and he said, "I'll call you tomorrow." I looked at him, and I thanked him for the beautiful night.

After that night, he took me out every night. Every now and then, we went to the beach at night with a bottle of champagne to talk, look at the stars, and hear the waves from the boardwalk.

Don took me to all the expensive restaurants in Queens, Brooklyn, and Manhattan. Octavio, Gloria's husband, got me a job at a restaurant, and Don came to the restaurant on his days off to see me, eat breakfast, and talk to me. When he would 'finish, he'd left me a $10 tip.

I worked at the restaurant to buy John clothes and supplies for school. My older son was working to buy his clothes and the things he needed for school. Don came to see me every night at Gloria's house.

One day, Gloria told me, "Amira, you have a good man, ask him to help you." I told Gloria, "Okay, I will talk to him." That afternoon, Don came to get me after he came from work, and he took me to the beach.

When we were walking on the boardwalk, I told Don that I could no longer stay at Gloria's apartment, and I started to cry. Don 'told me, "Don't you worry; tomorrow, I will come and get you. Get your stuff ready, because you will come to live with me. We stood there at the beach, looking at the sea and talking.

When we finished talking, he took me home, and I told Gloria that I had spoken with Don, and that he was going to take me to live with him. Gloria looked at me and said, "I wish you the best."

That night, I started to get my clothes ready. It wasn't much, because I had left everything behind when I lost the apartment. Don came to get me the next evening, and he took me to live with him in the basement of his father's house.

I was a little scared. In the beginning, Don's parents didn't know that I was staying in the basement. Don would wake up at 3:30 every morning to go to work, and I stayed in the basement by myself. But before Don's parents would wake up, I would leave the house and go to Sarah's apartment in the projects and stay there until Don finished work and picked me up, until one day, Don took me upstairs to his parents' apartment and told his mother, Lara, and his father, Jose, that I was staying with him in the basement.

I never had to hide again. His parents were very sweet to me. One day while Don was working, I went to a congressman's office to see if they could help me get a housing apartment. Another day, I went to speak with a social worker at the hospital about my younger son. I went to see her, to see if she could help me get an apartment, because my family was separated. The social worker sent John and me to talk with a psychiatrist for children.

The receptionist called John's name, and we went into the office to talk to the psychiatrist. I told the doctor that I had lost my apartment, and I wanted my family back together. Then the doctor told me to wait outside, because she wanted to talk with John.

I left the room, and the doctor stood in the office, talking with John for a while. When they finished talking, the doctor called me into the office, and she gave me two filled prescriptions for my son. She told me that she would get back to me, and I told her, "Okay, thank you."

I left the office, and while I was walking, I looked at the prescriptions that she had given me for my son, and I threw them in the garbage. My son didn't need drugs; we needed help with an apartment.

We left the office and we went to Sarah's apartment, and Don came to pick me up. Don started helping me to look for an apartment. He took me to a lot of real estate offices, but I didn't have any luck. I think it was because I wasn't working, but one day Rick called and told me that his girlfriend's grandmother had an apartment vacancy. I told my son to tell her that I was going to see the apartment in the afternoon.

I went to see the apartment with Don, and he asked me, "What do you think?" I told Don I had no other choice. I had to take it, and I told the owner of the building that I was going to take the apartment. And I moved to Hopkins Avenue, in Brooklyn, to a four-room apartment with John, and Don.

My other son was living with his girlfriend in the building, on the third floor. After we had lived there for a month, a man knocked on my door, and he introduced himself as a caseworker from a child abuse agency. I asked him, "What do you mean, child abuse? I never abuse my children." He told me that I went to talk to a social worker and asked her for help because I was on the street with my son. I told the man that it wasn't like that. My son was staying with my friend, Sarah, until I was able to find an apartment. That didn't mean I was abusing my son. The man told me that I had to go to the office to sign some papers.

I went to the office, and I told the man that I wasn't a bad mother, and to please help me with the mess that the social worker had made. And he told me not to worry, because I had my apartment already, and everything was clear. It didn't matter that I got the apartment; John stayed at Sarah's house, and she became like a mother to him.

Rick gave me a beautiful grandson. They named him Hen. I started going to agencies, looking for a job, and the Progress Agency found me one at the Department of Finance. It was nice, working for them.

After four years of living on that street, Don decided to get mee another apartment. Don went to the real estate office with me and signed his name to all the real estate papers in the offices we went to.

One day, one of the agents from the real estate office called me to tell me that he had a vacant apartment. I told the agent that my boyfriend, Don, was at work, but as soon he came home, we would go and see the apartment.

Don came home from work and we drove to Queens. We liked the apartment very much, and we told the agent that we would take it. We went to the office and gave them a month's rent and a month's security.

Don and I packed our clothes, took my living room set and my new refrigerator, and moved to the one-bedroom apartment. We slept on the sofa for a couple of days, until Don purchased an Italian bedroom set and a dining room from Simmon's.

After a couple of months, he purchased a new stove. After working for the Department of Finance for a year and a couple of months, they no longer needed me, and the agency got me another job with the school in Queens for the yellow buses.

I answered the telephone and took complaints from · parents about the drivers being late or not picking up their children. It was a different kind of complaint every day. Sometimes, the supervisor assigned me to work as a switchboard operator. To get to work, I would take the train every morning and get off at the same street. I started work at six o'clock in the morning; I would wake up at 3:30 in the morning to be on time for work. One morning, I got off at the same stop, and I. saw a man standing behind the wall. I got really scared, and when I got home, I told Don what had happened at the train station. He called transportation to see if it there was another way that I could go to work. The man from transportation told Don that I could take the M train, and transfer to the L train, then the F train going to Queens, and get off at the designated place – I think that was the street – and walk about two blocks. The new way was longer, but it was safer.

One day, I went to the doctor because I wasn't feeling well, and the doctor informed me I had a chronic condition, and I had to stop working. Don told me to stop working and stay home, that I didn't have to work, and that he would take care of me. I told him that I needed to work to pay my rent, and he told me he would help me with everything.

I stayed home for two years. After staying home for two years, I was feeling better, and I decided to look for a good job with medical insurance.

SEXUAL HARASSMENT IN THE POST OFFICE

I filled out applications for all the city jobs. I would buy the newspaper and look through the classifieds. I saw one for the postal service, and when Don came home, I told him I wanted to work for the post office. He told me that it was hard to get in, and that there were a lot of people waiting to be called. I told him again that I wanted to work for the post office, and that I had seen an advertisement in the *Daily News* about training in Manhattan. I told him that I was going to call them, no matter what Don told me.

I went to the office to get more information about the training. The man that was at the desk told me the course would cost me $400 dollars for a couple of weeks. I told the man that I would give him a call, and I left.

I called Don at his job, and I told him that they wanted me to pay $400 dollars for the training. He asked me, "What do you think?" I told him that if I paid that amount of money and I didn't pass the test, I would lose the money.

I called the man at the office and told him that I was not going to take the class, and that there must be another way. So, I went to the bookstore to look for the post office book, and I bought it. Every night, I read the book and timed myself. And I told some of my friends that if they knew about any post office giving the test, to call me or get me the application. I also bought the chief newspaper to see if they were giving the test.

One day, Stephanie called me and told me that David (my friend from New Jersey) was in her apartment. I went upstairs to see David. We started talking, and I told him that I was trying to get an application for the post office to take the test. He told me that the post office was going to give the test in New Jersey. I got really happy, and I told Don to get me the application.

When I went home, I told Don that they were going to give the test for the post office in New Jersey, and he told me it was too far from home. I told him that it was okay; that I was willing to travel, and he told me no, and to stay home.

No matter what, I still looked for the postal application, and,: one day, my best friend Kathy, from the South, called me and told me that they were giving applications to take the test at the post office in Brooklyn.

I drove over there and parked the car, and the line was all the way around the block. I waited in the line, and finally I got the application.

I went home, filled it out, and sent it in. They sent me an appointment to take the test in the Bronx, and Don drove me there. I took the test, and the questions were really easy. Then a couple of days passed, and they sent me a letter stating that I had passed the test and was on the waiting list.

But I didn't give up. I still looked for more applications. They sent me the appointment to take the test in Brooklyn. When I got there, I could not find any parking, and I said to a man from India, who was standing in front of a house, that I was going to take the test for the post office, and I could not find any parking. The man told me to park the car in front of his driveway.

I parked the car and told the man, "Thank you," and I ran, because I was three blocks away from where I was going to take the test, and I didn't want to be late. I took the test and waited for the results.

One day, Don told me to meet him in front of the post office where he worked to go for lunch. I waited in the lobby, and I went to the postal police and asked a man where the office was, to see if they were giving applications to take the test for the post office. He told me it was on the side of the building.

I went there and got another application, and I filled out the application right there and sent it in. When Don came to get me to have lunch, I told him that I got another application, and he told me again, "Baby, they're not going to call you." And I told him, "Yes, they will call me."

One day, I received the score from the test that I took in Brooklyn: I passed. When Don came home from work, I showed him the letter, and he told me not to get my hopes too high; that I wasn't the only one taking the test. When he told me that, I told him, "One day you will be surprised."

Every night, before I went to sleep, I prayed, asking God to please help me get the job at the post office.

One afternoon, I went to see if I had gotten any mail, and when I opened the mailbox I saw a letter from the post office with my name on it. I opened it and, sure enough, it was the letter from the postal service, a call-in notice for an interview. I had been put on their registration for employment. I was so happy, I said loudly, "Thank you, Lord, for giving me the job."

My appointment was for July 9, 1998, at eight o'clock in the morning. My position would be mail handler.

When I got to the post office, there were a lot of people there for the interview. A man gave us a tour of the facility, telling us about the machines and the barcodes. He showed us where we were going to take the lifting test. When he finished giving us the tour, he told us to go to the medical unit to get a drug screening test and a physical examination. The nurse took my urine and gave me a form to fill out, asking questions about my health. I filled out the form, and then the nurse told me they were going to get back to me by mail, and to go for a lifting test on the third floor. When I got to the lifting area, there was a man who told us that we had to put all the bags that were on the skid, which was filled with bags, inside the other empty skid, a couple of feet away.

In the beginning, when it was my turn to do the lifting, it was okay, but lifting the bags from one side to the other made them feel heavier. The last bag was so heavy that I dropped it when I got between the two skids. The man told me, "Cojela por el medio," to grab it in the middle, so I did, and I got to the other side and put it on top of the other bags.

When I finished the lifting, I went outside and told Don all that I had done inside, and we went home.

After a week, I received a letter stating the day I was going to start orientation: August 1, 1998.

That day, they put all of us in a room, and management came to talk to us about the rules of the post office: discrimination, sexual harassment, the ninety days of probation, insurance, etc. We had orientation for a week, and then I started working as a mail handler on probation for ninety days.

After working for the postal service for twenty-seven days, a 204-B supervisor named Samantha started pushing the flexes to work faster. I was trying to work faster because I didn't want to lose my job, and I banged my left elbow against the metal railing. The pain was so bad that I went down to the floor, telling the supervisor I was hurt, and the supervisor yelled, "Faster!" I told her, "You come up here and do it faster."

I came down from my working area, holding my elbow, and I told the supervisor that I wanted to go to the hospital. She told me that I had to make an accident report. So, I did, and I went to see Dr. Parr from the medical unit of the post office.

I told him what had happened, and he asked me if I could keep working. I told him that I was in a lot of pain, and I wanted to go to the hospital near where I lived. The doctor sent me home.

I left and went to the hospital in Queens. I was out of work for a couple of days. I went to see the doctor at the medical unit to clear me. When I showed him my arm, which was black and blue, he told me he had thought that I was faking my injury when I went to see him on the day of my accident. I told the doctor I wasn't a faker.

After fifteen days, early one morning I went to work with a bad pain in my right side that was taking over my leg, and I could not walk quickly.

I told Mr. Nixon, my supervisor, and he sent me to the medical unit, and the doctor sent me home, "Not fit for duty." The doctor stated: *Employee in significant discomfort. Request to follow-up with Amiras medical doctor (medical Concur). Has been given a work limitation form to provide in advance of any work return allowance. Should be seen by the medical unit MD before any physical work return is permitted or resumed.*

Dr. Perkins gave me a letter to take to my doctor, and the work-limitation form, for him to fill it out, and I went to my doctor the same day. He filled out the light-duty form.

He gave me an appointment to go and see him in four days. I went to see my doctor for an evaluation, and he asked me if I was feeling any better. I said yes, I could return to work. The next day, I went to see the medical unit doctor, and he put me on light duty.

One day, I went to my doctor for medical results, and the doctor told me that I had to get surgery. I told the doctor, "Please, not now." I had just started working for the postal service, and I was on a ninety-day probation period. The doctor told me that I had to have the surgery as soon as possible. I told him, "Okay." I had only been working for one month and a couple of weeks before I went in for surgery.

My appointment for surgery was for September 29, 1998. I went Lack lo work after a few days.

When I got to my working area, I looked for Mr. Nixon, and I gave him my documentation. He accepted it. And I went to my working area and started working. I was feeling sick with fever. A lady passed through my working area and asked me, "What it is wrong with you? If you feel sick, go home."

SEXUAL HARASSMENT IN THE POST OFFICE

I went to the restroom, and I was bleeding a lot. I looked in the mirror. My eyes were really red. I came out of the restroom, and I went to talk to my supervisor. I told him that I was feeling weak and that I needed to take a couple of days off, because I had just had surgery. He told me that I was on probation, and it was going to interfere with my career. I told him that my health came first. He looked at me and told me okay, and sent me to the medical unit to see Dr. Perkins. The doctor wasn't in, so I spoke to the nurse and told her about what had happened with my surgery. She advised: *PMD if sx persist NFFD BOT*, meaning, "Medical doctor if symptoms persist, not fit for duty balance of tour."

I went to my doctor, and I told him that I had had to leave work a week (and I told him why I had left the job). He gave me a letter for being absent, and the next day I went to work and I gave the letter to Mr. Nixon. He accepted it.

One day before my ninety days was up, one of the manager distribution operators named Mr. Dorman, "the boss from the floor," gave me an envelope while I was working. He left and I opened it, and it was my discharge letter, dated October 27, 1998, removing me from the post office.

My heart stopped beating, and I was in shock. I didn't know what to do. I was ashamed that he had given me that letter in front of my coworkers. I said to myself, *This can't be happening.*

I left the working floor to look for Mr. Dorman. I saw him, and I ran after him, asking him, "What is this letter about?" He said, "Come with me to my office."

In the office, he told me to sit down. He started to read the letter. When he was reading the letter to me, it made me very upset. He asked me why I had been absent for six days. I told him that I was sick with a bad rash around my back and stomach that caused me pain on my left leg, and also because I had had surgery and a woman problem, and I was bleeding too much. He asked me, "Why were you on light duty?" I told him that I had been sick. I asked Mr. Dorman, "If my evaluation was satisfactory from my supervisor, why am I getting this letter?" He told me that Mr. Nixon was not supposed to give me my evaluation; that it was supposed to be Nicole or Mr. Green. I told Mr. Dorman that my supervisor evaluated me for three months, and that the senior plant manager didn't know how to organize his people. Mr. Dorman told me he did not sign the discharge letter, and that it was the senior plant manager, Dustin Hoffman. I asked him where I could find the senior plant manager, and he told me to check the third floor.

I went up to the third floor and told the receptionist that I would like to speak to the senior plant manager, Mr. Morris. The receptionist asked me if I had an appointment, and I told her, "The way that I feel, I don't need an appointment to see him." She told me to speak to the other plant manager, Mr. Strobel, but he wasn't in his office. I told the receptionist I'd be back, and I went downstairs to look for my belongings. One of my coworkers told me that Mr. Dorman, the one who gave me the termination letter, and Nicole, were looking for me. But they saw me and called me to the office.

Mr. Dorman told me, "I don't think you understood what I said to you before." I said to him, "I understood everything you said to me, so if you're not going to give me back my job, I don't want to hear it." I left the office and went back to the third floor. I asked the receptionist if Mr. Strobel was in his office, and she told me yes, to go into his office.

When I went inside his office, he told me to have a seat, and I said to him, "I would like to have my check, because I'm leaving." He said, "I can mail it to you." He gave me an envelope and I took out my pen, and while I was writing my address on the envelope, I asked him, "Why did you terminate me? Because I was sick?" And he told me that it was the regulation for the post office. I told him I had gotten sick and could not help it. He said, "You only had a minor surgery." I said I had been bleeding to death, and he told me that on the probation period I could not be absent. I told him once again that I had been sick, and he told me that I had been sick for too many days, and I said, "I can't stop nature. You get sick, everyone gets sick." He told me, "I opened a little door for you to come in [meaning that I came to work for the post office] and you couldn't come through it." And I told him, "And I have a big door, and you can't come through it." I thanked him, and I left his office.

I was discharged from the postal service, effective at the close of business, October 29, 1998. The reasons for the discharge were *Work Performance and Unsatisfactory Attendance.*

The evaluation report for eighty days was received, and it was determined that my attendance and work performance were unsatisfactory, and that I had been hired for the position of mail handler, and was assigned to the linear sorter. I had been on light duty since September 10, 1998, working without the knowledge and authorization of the manager of distribution operations on the loose flat sorter. I had not demonstrated the ability for satisfactorily performing mail handling duties and functions. The proper rating for the factor was revised to unacceptable. I had been absent or did not complete my tour of duty on six occasions: *September 10, 1998, 4.02 hours sick leave without pay (LWOP); September 11, 1998, 8.00 hours of sick leave (LWOP); September 12, 1998, 8.00 hours of sick leave (LWOP); September 13, 1998, 8.00 hours of sick leave (LWOP) September 24, 1998 5.00 hours of sick leave (LWOP); October 02, 1998 6.00 sick leave (LWOP).*

    I went to Mr. Nixon and told him about my letter, and he told me that his boss had called him to his office and asked him, "Why did you give her satisfactory on her evaluation? Why? Because she is Puerto Rican?" I asked him why he said that, and he just got quiet. I told my supervisor that I was leaving. While I went through the front doors, a coworker stopped me and told me to go and speak with Mr. Batista. It didn't matter, because I wasn't a member of the union. I went to speak to Mr. Brillo, the President from Local-1, and I told him about my problem and asked him for help. Mr. Brillo told me to write down everything that happened, and to fax it to him. I said to him, "Okay," and I left work and drove home. When I got home, I wrote my statement.

STATEMENT 1

On September 10, 1998

I went to work with bad pain in my right leg. I clocked in at 6:00 a.m. I saw my supervisor, Mr. Nixon, and he asked me what was wrong, I said I didn't know, but I had pain on my right side and could not walk, and I wanted to go to the medical unit. Mr. Nixon told me that Dr. Perkins would be in at 9:00 a.m. Meanwhile, I went to my working floor from 6:00 a.m. to 8:45 a.m. I was working in severe pain. I went to see Mr. Nixon, and I told him I could not stand the pain. He gave me a note to take to the medical unit. I went to see Dr. Perkins, and he checked me for a hernia and asked me if I wanted to go home or stay. I said to him that I wanted to see my own doctor. I went to see my doctor; and he gave me painkillers and told me to stay home.

I have enclosed copies of medical reports.

STATEMENT 2

On October 2, 1998, I went to work bleeding a lot. I clocked in at 6:00 a.m. I saw Mr. Nixon, and I told him that I was feeling sick. He told me not to leave. I told him that I was going to try to hang in there, but while I was working, I was feeling hot, like I had a fever. I went to the ladies' room and looked at myself in the mirror and asked myself what was wrong with me and started to cry. I went to see Mr. Nixon, and I told him that I wanted to see Dr. Perkins. He said the doctor was not in that day. I asked if the nurse was in. I said to him that I needed to go home; I needed to rest, I was bleeding too much. Mr. Nixon gave me the medical form, and I went to the medical unit. I spoke to the nurse, and I told her that I was bleeding a lot and wanted to go home. She gave me a medical release to go home. I never should have gone to work, but I was on probation, and I was afraid I would lose my job. That day, I drove from work, and it took me one hour to get home.

STATEMENT 3

November 1, 1998

On my second evaluation that I signed, with a satisfactory rating, which was given to me by my supervisor, Mr. Nixon, he told me I wasn't going to keep my job after my ninety days, because of my absences. I told him that I got sick, something I had no control over. He said, "I'm just telling you." I was very upset.

On my third evaluation that I signed, with a satisfactory rating, he told me that his boss was going to talk to him about why he gave me a satisfactory on my evaluation. I told Mr. Nixon that my absences were due to my sickness. I was never late, not even once, while I was on my probation for three months, and was traveling a long distance. I said to him that my work performance was excellent. He said to me, "They are going to call you." I said I would not lie about my sickness.

Mr. Nixon told me that they had called him. I asked him what happened. He said that someone upstairs had asked him, "Why did you gave her satisfactory, if she was absent so much, because you are the same race?"

Sincerely,
Amira

STATEMENT 4

November 1, 1998

This is a list of the people that I would like present at my hearing:

Bosses	Supervisors	Loose Flat Belt Workers
Mr. Strobel	Mr. Nixon	Lucy
Mr. Dorman Mr. Morris	Nicole (Supervisor)	Arnel
	Samantha (204-B)	Andrew
	Mr. Green (Supervisor)	Leon

I filed a grievance for removal based on racial discrimination on October 29, 1998, and I faxed it to Mr. Batista.

Sincerely,
Amira

REQUEST FOR INFORMATION

I am requesting the following documents and witnesses be made available in order to property identify whether or not a grievance does exist, and if so, their relevancy to the grievant.
Copy of grievant's monthly evaluation for ninety-day probation.
Copy of 3972, with all documentation provided.

Amira

SEXUAL HARASSMENT IN THE POST OFFICE

After a month or so, Mr. Brillo sent me the two letters that he had sent to the senior plant manager in charge.

One day, management assigned a supervisor named Thomas Lawrence to the machines. Thomas was very unprofessional with the other workers, except with his friends. A couple of times, Thomas talked to me, very nastily.

I came to work one day, and Thomas asked me what time I started working. I told him, "At 5:00 p.m." I went to my working area and sat down on the chair, and Thomas came to me and said, "Your break is not going to be a half-hour. It is going to be fifteen minutes or twenty minutes." I said, "Okay." Then I asked him if that fifteen or twenty minutes was for everyone. He said, "Worry about yourself." I said to him, "I am worried about myself." And then I was quiet.

At five o'clock, I clocked in, and Thomas assigned me· to work on machine number seven, with my co-worker and friend, Michael. Thomas came up to machine number seven and started looking; I began to work with Michael (I was on the sweep side), and Michael said to me that the machine was making a noise like there were birds inside. I smiled and opened the door to the machine to see what was wrong. Thomas told me to close the door to the machine. I told him that he needed to call the mechanic. In a harsh tone, he told me again to close the door. I closed the door.

He left and called the mechanic. The mechanic came to see what was wrong with the machine. Thomas came back to the machine. I told the mechanic about the noise that the machine was making. He opened the top door, and I pointed to a piece of paper caught in the belt of the machine. Thomas told me, with a bad tone, to take my hand away from there, but when the mechanic came to fix something on the machine, I had to show him where the problem was. Then Thomas, with the same tone, told me, "Amira, come, you're going to prime." That meant I would be sorting mail in another location. I said okay, and I smiled.

He took my badge and moved me to the prime aisle. I sat down and started working. He left and came back with all of my belongings and gave them to me. I just looked at him, and didn't say anything when he gave them to me. I started to work, and Kara, a 204-B supervisor, saw me working at prime and asked me, "Amira, what are you doing here?" I told her that Thomas was acting strangely. And she said that she needed me to work for her, but she was going to ask Tina, the acting MDO in charge, when she came back from the office.

After a couple of minutes, Kara came back to the aisle and told the supervisor from the prime aisle, Mrs. Manson, that she was going to take me. Everything was okay. I was working on the flip-flop. Kara came to me and asked me to release someone on machine number four on the OCR.

I started to work on the OCR at about 7:55 p.m. I can't remember who went to work with me, but I was on the sweep side. Then, I heard a loud voice calling me, "Amira, Amira!" I turned my head really slowly, and it was Thomas.

He moved his head twice, calling me, licking his lips, with his legs wide open. I got scared and said no, and then I went to Kara and told her that Thonmas was calling me to work at the DBCS machine. Kara told me that was okay. I told her that, after I finished working, I was going to take my lunch at 8:30, and she said okay, and to come back to her. I said to her, "I'll see you later."

I started working on machine number five by myself, and then Louise came to work with me. At 8:20, Louise left the machine and went to lunch. And at 8:25, I went to the restroom to wash up. When I was coming out of the restroom, Thomas was paging me to work area J-4.

I went to the work area, and he asked me where I was going. I said to him that I was going to take my lunch. He said to me, "Come! Let's go to see Manson, to see if she knows you are going to lunch." I said to Thomas, "I am not working for Manson, I am working for Kara." Then, with a bad tone in his voice and an equally bad attitude, he said, "When I move you to a different location, you can't move from there until I tell you so. I put you there for a reason." I told him, "I don't belong to anyone in the post office. Kara needed me, so I went to work for her." He asked me if Kara knew I was going to take my lunch, and I said yes.

Anyway, he went to see Manson, and I went, too. While they were talking, I said to both of them, "I am going to lunch." I went to the cafeteria, and all my friends were there: Martha, Louise, and others. I went to heat up my food and sat down. I told my friends that Thomas was acting strangely to me. And they asked me, "What's wrong with your eyes?" I said, "I don't know." While I was eating, in front of all my friends and everyone else in the cafeteria, Thomas came in, and with a bad tone in his voice, said, "Amira, come." I told him, "I am eating." And he said to me, "If you don't want to come, you will see!" My friend Martha told me, "Amira, go, see what he wants." I told Martha, "Please, I am eating." She said to me, "Baby, I know."

I started shaking, and my stomach got upset, and I left my food on the table. I told my friends to excuse me, and I walked after Thomas. Thomas walked to the management conference room. He started talking to me, and said he had called Kara to see if she knew where I was, and she said she didn't know. I told him, "You know I take my lunch at 8:30." Then he told me that he needed me at another machine. I told him that he didn't tell me about going to another machine. We came out of the conference room, and he said, "I am going to call Kara, to see if she knew you were taking your lunch, and if she said no, you're going to see." I was just listening to those words, and then I told him, "I would like to finish my food." He said, "No. I need you at the machine." Then he said, "Let's go and get a shop steward. Now come on!"

I got really nervous, and I didn't follow him. I went back to the cafeteria and told my friends that he had a bad attitude. I started crying, and I left and went to the ATAL room. I told Mrs. Claribel (the secretary in charge) I needed to see the MDO, "Now." I was crying and shaking. Mrs. Claribel told me that Tina, the assistant MDO, had gone to lunch. Tasked her again, "Where is she? I need to talk to her now.". Mrs. Claribel told me that she was outside, getting lunch.

I left the ATAL room, and I went to look for Beth, the shop steward. Thomas started paging me over and over: "Amira, come to J-4." I went to the flat sorter, and my friend, Jeffrey, saw me and asked me, "Amira, what's wrong?" I was crying, and I told Jeffrey I needed to talk to Beth, and he told me that he was going to help me look for her, and I walked over to see my best friend, Lou, and when he saw me, he asked me, "Who put you like that?" I told Lou, "Thomas." "I don't know what's wrong with him."

Thomas started paging me all over again, and Lou told me to call him back. I said, "No, please, no." Then I left to look for Beth (I couldn't find her), and I went back to Lou, and he told me that he had called Thomas and told him I was looking for a shop steward, and that Thomas got an attitude with him. Thomas told Lou that it wasn't his business. Lou told him, "Don't get an attitude with me, I'm just doing you a favor."

While I was talking to Lou, Jeffrey came to me and told me that Beth was in the break room, having lunch. I went to see Beth, and she was on her lunch break. I said, "Beth, I am sorry to bother you on your lunch break, but I need to talk to you." I started to cry.

Beth stopped eating and took me for a walk; I told her everything that Thomas did to me. She told me to get the MDO. I told her that the MDO had gone outside to get lunch. I told Beth I wanted to go home; she told me to get a 3971 form and come back to her.

When I went to the ATAL room to get the form, Tina was there. I asked her for a 3971, and I told her I was looking for her. And she told me, "Thomas needs you at the machine." She could not see that I was very upset and shaking. Instead of asking me, "Amira, what is wrong?" she told me to go back to the machine and work for Thomas.

I told her to wait, and I went to get Beth. I told Beth that Tina was in the office, and we went to see her. Tina took us to the conference room, and I told Tina a little of what Thomas was doing to me. I was crying hysterically, and I told her that I wanted to go home. She told me that I couldn't go home, because Thomas needed me on the machine, and I filled out the 3971, stating: *Not feeling well due to severe stress from my supervisor Mr. Thomas Lawrence.*

I gave it to her; she disapproved of it, "pending documentation." I went home, and I called the 800 number to make a complaint against Thomas Lawrence.

After ten days, the Complaint Organization Department, the COD, sent me a form to make the complaint. I wrote that the persons involved were *Supervisor Thomas Lawrence, and the MDO, Mr. Fernando*. Mr. Fernando didn't have anything to do with the problem, but I wrote his name so he would help me, because he was the boss from Tour-3.

I sent the form, and they made me an appointment for Thursday, June 1, 2000, at five o'clock in the afternoon.

When I got there, I went to the management conference room with my representative, Beth. I introduced myself to the mediator, who was the person to solve the problem, and who didn't work for the post office. Mr. Fernando and Thomas came into the room, and the mediator told us that we were going to have a chance to talk to her in private, and the counselee, who was me, was going to start talking first.

I started to tell the mediator and Mr. Fernando what Thomas had done on the working floor. Then Thomas was to share his point of view. The mediator asked them to come back in ten minutes so that she could talk to me.

They left, and I told the mediator that what Thomas was really doing to me was sexual harassment. I told her about the time that he licked his lips, with his legs wide open, and the way that he was looking at me, and that the way he was talking to me was "harassing." I told her that I didn't write about the sexual harassment because I didn't want to lose my job or for him to lose his job. I said to her that Thomas needed to get some classes to deal with people around him. The mediator told me to write an apology letter to Thomas, and I told her that I could not write an apology, because I didn't do anything wrong to him. I told her that he was the one who needed to write an apology letter to me. The mediator told Beth and me to wait outside, and she called Thomas and Mr. Fernando into the room. When I came inside the room, the mediator had an apology letter from Thomas.

I settled the case with Thomas. Mr. Fernando moved Thomas to the flat sorter machine and told him not to be around me. He left me working on the machines. After that day, I never saw Thomas around my working floor again.

One day, I wrote a letter to Mr. Fernando, because I wanted to become a 204-B supervisor. Mr. Fernando replied to my letter, stating that they presently had a number of employees who had been trained and were used during vacation periods and supervisors' SDOs. My application was rejected.

Something happened, Mr. Fernando left the facility, and a new MDO, Mr. Johnson, came to work in the facility.

One day, while I was working on number eight, Mr. Johnson came to my working area and told me to work the flat sorter. I told him that I could not work under Thomas's supervision. He asked me why, and I told him that it was because I had taken him to COD, and Mr. Fernando had stationed him away from me, and he said to me that he was going to talk to Mrs. Jane, an MDO.

He left, and came back to my working area, and told me that she didn't know anything about it. (She lied, because she knew about the case with me and Thomas.) He asked me if I had any paper stating I could not work for Thomas, and I told him that the only paper I had was a copy of the settlement. He told me to bring them, and that he would like to see them.

The next day, when I went to work, I gave Mr. Johnson the papers to read, and he took them. Minutes later, Mrs. Jane called me to the ATAL. When I went to the ATAL, present were Mr. Johnson, Mrs. Jane, and Thomas.

Mrs. Jane started by saying that I could work with Thomas, and I told her that I could not work under his supervision. If she wanted to know the reason, then she could ask him. The only thing that I knew was that Mr. Fernando had kept us apart, so as not to be around each other. Mrs. Jane, with a smile on her face, and making faces, told me, "Well, Fernando is not here anymore." And I told her, "I will not work under his supervision." Thomas was listening and smiling.

I left the room and went to my working area. I didn't work under Thomas's supervision.

One morning, I woke up and my kidneys were acting up. I took a shower, and I told Don (he was off that day) that I wanted to go to the emergency room, because of my kidneys.

He got dressed really fast and drove me to the hospital. At the emergency room, they did bloodwork, and I asked the nurse to give me something for the pain, but she told me that I had to wait for the blood results to come back.

When the results came back, they gave me an injection for the pain and an IV, and they left me in the emergency room for observation. They discharged me from the hospital the next afternoon.

The doctor from the emergency room told me to follow up with my medical doctor. I went to see my doctor, and he wrote a letter to take to work.

At the postal service, sometimes we had to work on our days off, but in my situation I could not work on my days off, and I was having trouble with management. I told them that, on my days off, I made appointments to see my doctor. But the only thing that they said to me was, "You are a flex [meaning part-time, flexible employee], and you have to work on your days off."

The next day, I called the doctor's office and made an appointment to see him. When I went to see my doctor on my appointment date, I told him that management was trying to make me do overtime, and he wrote a letter to give to management.

Sonia Sanchez came to work for the facility to work as an MDO in the position that Mr. Fernando had left. While I was waiting to end my tour, I saw Sonia and introduced myself to her, but it was time for me to end my tour, and I said to her, "Nice meeting you," then I ended my tour and went home.

Another day, I gave a letter from my doctor to Sonia, and with an attitude she told me that I couldn't work for the post office, and to leave the facility. I just looked at her, went out of the room, and looked for Bob, a good shop steward from the union.

I told him my problem with Sonia, and he went to talk to her. With an attitude, she told Bob that I wouldn't work there anymore, and that I should leave the post office. I told Bob, "Okay, I am leaving." He told me that he was going to call me.

I left the room and went home. The next day, Bob called me to tell me that he'd filed a grievance. A few days later, I received another call from the shop steward, telling me that I could come back to work, and I told him that I wasn't going to work until Sonia called me and asked me to return to work, because what she did wasn't professional.

After eight days, Sonia called me at home. She said, "Amira, it is time for you to come back to work. We need you here." I told her, "Okay, I'll be there tomorrow," and I hung up the telephone. I called Bob, really fast, and I told him that I had just spoken to Sonia. _And he said to me that Sonia had made an agreement. I told him to fax it to me, so he did, and when I got the fax I started reading it.

When Don came home, I showed him the agreement letter, and the next day T returned for duty.

One day, Richard Thorne came to work for the postal service as a supervisor. Richard was very rude to all of our coworkers. A couple of times, guys almost had fights with him in the working area. He also had a big argument with a female coworker, and he was in her face, screaming at her.

Every day, Richard looked at me and the way I was dressed for work. One day, he watched me and threatened me. He told me about the dress code, and I asked him, "What is wrong with it? I am dressed okay." I had on a spaghetti-strap dress with a shirt underneath, and he told me that I wasn't appropriately dressed for work. I asked him again why not, and he told me that he was going to take me off the clock.

I went to get the union representative, Bob, at the express mail location. I told Bob that Richard was going to take me off the clock because of my dress, and he asked me, "What is wrong with the way that you are dressed?" I told him, "I don't know, ask him, please."

We went to the postal, and Bob asked Richard what was wrong with my dress. Richard told him that I wasn't appropriately dressed for work, that he had ended my tour, and that I could go home. I looked at Bob, walked away, and left.

When, I got home, Don asked me, "Baby, what's wrong, are you okay?" I told him what had happened, and he told me everything was going to be all right. I just looked at him, and I went to take a shower. When I finished taking the shower, I told Don, "I am going to bed."

The next day, I went back to work. A couple of my friends came, dressed in spaghetti-strap shirts, and Richard didn't say anything to them.

Another day, I clocked in at four o'clock in the afternoon, and Richard told me to go to machine number ten and work with Martha. At about 8:40 p.m., I told Martha that I was going to the restroom. She said okay, and about 8:50 p.m., I left the restroom, and Richard was standing next to the machine that I was working on.

When I saw him, he was staring at me from a distance, with a terrible look in his eyes. I just walked and passed next to him, and he didn't say anything to me.

At about 10:05 p.m., Martha told me, "Amira, I need some fresh air," and I told her, "Me too, I am sweating." We cleaned the stackers, and I told Martha, "Go and get some fresh air." She told me, "No, you go first." I said to her, "Okay."

While I was walking, I was looking back and talking to her, and I told her, "I'll be right back." When I made a right turn, I heard a voice calling me, "Amira, Amira" I turned my head slowly, and saw that it was Richard. I said to him, "Yes?" He told me with an attitude, *"Go back to your machine."* I looked at him and I said, "Excuse me?" And he said, with a strong voice, *"Go to your machine now."* I told him that I was going to get some fresh air, and he told me, "Go, go." But while I was walking, he was behind me, saying, "Control yourself, or you will see."

I got scared, and I started to walk faster, because there wasn't anyone around us. When I got to the machine, I started to load the ledge with mail, and he stood next to my machine, number nine, and told me the same thing, but in Spanish, "Controlate oh tu vas a ver." He told me that he was watching me, and that I had gone to the restroom, took five minutes, and that the machine was running with only one operator. I got angry and told him twice to get off my back, or that I would take him to Complaint Organization Department (COD). He told me, "Oh, you don't like to listen."

Then he walked away from the machine. One of my coworkers saw me and asked what was wrong, and I told her. Then I went to the union office and made a Grievance Statement, and when I got home, I called the COD to make a complaint against him.

On July 26, 2001, Richard called me to the conference room, and I called a steward. He gave me a letter of warning. It was an official disciplinary letter warning against behavior unbecoming of a postal, and unauthorized absence from work.

When he told me the reason for the letter of warning, I got really nervous, because everything that he wrote in the letter was a lie. What they wanted to do was ruin my reputation and my job. He told me to sign the letter; I refused. I asked to go home, because all the tension had gotten me upset. I went to the ATAL room and got a 3971 form to go home. The shop steward gave me a DC-12 form for compensation, which he asked Richard for, to take to my doctor.

One day, I was working on machine number seven, and Richard stood behind my back and said, "Amira, the shirt." I looked at him, and I left the machine and looked for the MDO, Sonia. I saw Sonia talking to Rita, and I went to her and asked her, "Sonia, please tell me, what is wrong with my clothing?" And she said, "Nothing." I told her, "Then tell something to Richard, because he is behind my back all the time." And she said, "Amira, that is love." I just looked at her and told her I needed fresh air, and she said, "Yes, go and take some air."

Walking to the back, I talked loudly to myself, "Oh my God, this is serious, and she took it as a joke; what is wrong with her?"

When I got home, I called the COD and filed a complaint against Richard for harassment. I got sick because of all the things that Richard was doing to me.

On August 2, 2001, I went to work after being stressed out for one week by Supervisor Richard. I went to my working area, and I told Margaret, the 204-B supervisor, that I was going to the union, because I could not work under Richard's supervision. She told me it was okay. I went to the union and spoke with the shop steward about the harassment, stalking, and threatening that Richard was responsible for. That was an everyday thing. I asked our shop steward to page Sonia, Richard's boss, and tell her to change me from my working area until I got my appointment with the COD.

Sonia took almost an hour to respond. She told our shop steward that she wasn't going to change me from my working area, because every place that she put me to work, I got into trouble, and then she hung up the phone. I told Tom to call her back, because it was a serious matter. Then she set up a meeting in the management conference room. I told Sonia that Richard had a problem with me. I told her, "The only thing that I am asking you is to change me to a different area until I get my COD appointment."

She got furious, and she started yelling at me, "No, no, no. COD is not going to come here and move my people." I got nervous and told her, "This is not the first time that I told you about Richard stalking me, checking my clothes, and threatening me, but you turned your back on me and because of you, the matter has gotten worse. And what you said to me was that it was love, and you laughed at me." Every time that I talked to her, she changed the subject. She asked me, with a bad tone in her voice, "What did you come here for?" I started to shake, and I asked her again, "Help me with my problem." She said, "Every place that I put you, you get in trouble." And she told me about the problem that I had with Thomas. I told her, "You weren't here when that happened. Don't change the subject." But with the way she was looking at me and talking to me, I started to cry. I felt a pain in my chest, and I could not talk or stand up. I felt like I was going to pass out. I just said in my mind, *Please, God, help me stand up and get out of here.*

Then I got up from the chair, and my legs could not hold my body. I walked to the ATAL room, and I heard a voice saying, "Oh my God, don't tell me that they made you like that in this place." When I looked, it was Doris, the receptionist, talking to me. I just started to shake more, and I got really scared, because I felt like I was going to faint. I told Doris, "Please, help me." She asked me, "Tell me, who do you want me to call to help you?" The only name that came out of my mouth was Louise, my friend, and then I said Margaret, a 204-B supervisor. Margaret came to the ATAL, and when she saw me, she kept moving her head, "No, no." I told her, "I can't no more." Margaret took me away from the ATAL, and I told her, "Margaret, the nurse." Then she took me to the medical unit to see the nurse.

I told the nurse what had happened, and she was shocked, because she had never seen me like that. She said, "You are always happy and smiling." The nurse filled out a medical form, stating it was job-related, and gave me a copy, and Margaret took me outside to get fresh air. My friend, Louise, came outside, and she told me, "Amira, this place is going to make you sick." And I told her, "Why me? I just want someone to help me." Louise said to me, let's go back upstairs to talk to Shop Steward Pauline, so she can get you the form to fill out for a job-related injury.

We saw Pauline, Louise told her my problem, and Pauline called Sonia to ask her for the form. Sonia told her to meet her in the conference room. When we got there, Sonia was sitting, waiting for us. We sat, and Sonia gave me the form. I told Pauline to fill out the form for me, and while she was filling out the form I started talking to Sonia. "I told you before about this problem, and all you did was laugh and tell me that it was love." She got really furious and screamed at me in front of the steward. "You're a liar. I didn't tell you that; you are crazy." Then she asked me, "How did Richard stress you out today? You didn't work with him." I told her, "Now it is you who is stressing me out," and Pauline said to me, "Amira, you have to sign here," and while I was preparing to sign the form, Sonia rushed us, saying, "Hurry up! I have 400 people to take care of, and Amira is wasting my time." I signed the form, and Pauline said, "Amira, wait, you have to get a copy of this form." Sonia, with a mean tone in her voice, said, "No, no, I don't have time for that."

And I left the conference room without a copy of the form that I had signed. I filled out a 3971 Request form for Notification of Absence, due to job-related stress, and I went home.

I called EPA and made an appointment to talk about the things that were happening to me at work. I went to EPA for almost two months, and she sent me to see a counselor. I went to see the counselor, and I had couple of visits before she saw me too stressed, and she sent me to see a psychologist. While going to EPA, and the counselor, I was going to my doctor, too, because I didn't trust going to EPA. I always thought that EPA was with the postal service, not with the employee. I went to my doctor, and I told him that the woman from EPA had sent me to see another doctor. I told him that I needed something to calm me down, but I didn't trust any doctor to prescribe me medication for stress. He gave me a prescription to calm me down, and he wrote a letter to take to my supervisor.

August 20, 2001, I went to see my doctor for my evaluation, and she gave me another letter.

When I went back to work, I started asking people to write letters for me, and some did. All the employees on the work floor were talking about the things that Richard was doing wrong, and how Sonia wasn't doing anything about it.

On September 4, 2001, the Labor Board Agency sent me a letter. The Employee Standards Association Office sent a letter to my doctor, too. They advised my doctor that I had filed a claim for compensation, claiming that I had sustained a job-related injury. They stated that the information submitted to their office to date was insufficient to establish the nature of my injury and its relationship to the factors of my employment. They requested a comprehensive report containing some information they requested, such as dates of examination and treatment; history of injury given to the physician; a detailed description of findings; results of all x-rays and laboratory tests; and diagnoses and clinical course of the treatments that followed.

They also asked for the physician's opinion, supported by a medical explanation, as to how the specific work incident, rather than a non-work related chronic medical condition, caused or aggravated the claimed injury. They stated that the explanation was crucial to a proper adjudication of the claim. They said that an opinion which is speculative or unsupported by clinical findings or test results could not be considered probative and may cause the denial of the claim. They gave us thirty days to submit all required documents.

On September 11, 2001, at 3:45 p.m., I went to see my psychologist.

On my pay period, 18-01, I got my pay stub. I was calling in sick, using my own time, and I wasn't getting paid. I called the union president, and I asked him to please find out what was going on.

The COD sent me a letter, setting up an appointment for Wednesday, September 19, 2001, at 6:00 p.m. When we all were inside the room, the mediator introduced herself and asked how we would like to be called, by our last names, or first names? I told her that she could call me Amira. She asked this of Richard and Beth, but when she asked Sonia what she would like to be called, she responded, with an attitude, "Whatever." The mediator was surprised with the answer that the boss gave her. And I started to tell the mediator the problem with Richard, and that after I told him that I was going to take him to COD, he gave me a letter of warning. I said that I wanted my name to be clean; that I didn't talk that way to a person, especially on my job; that I could not work under Supervisor Richard's supervision; and that he needed to be changed to another location. I also mentioned that Richard needed to go to training to deal and be professional with other people. I took some of my clothes with me, to show the mediator the way I was dressed when Richard told me about the dress code. Sonia and Richard were there when I told her that.

The mediator asked Richard and Sonia to step out for a couple of minutes, because she wanted to talk to me. I told the mediator that I had letters from other employees, and I showed them to her. She called Sonia and Richard into the room, and the mediator told Sonia the things I wanted: 1) Letter of warning removed; 2) To go back to the machine, under another supervisor, as long as Richard wasn't there; 3) Forty-five days of pay that were never received; 4) A letter of apology from Sonia for not helping when I needed help, calling me a liar, and calling me crazy; 5) Cooperation from Sonia when I ·went to her for help. I asked Sonia to remove my letter of warning, because what the letter was saying was not true. She told me no. I was, unfortunately, unable to resolve the dispute with Sonia through the COD process.

The mediator asked me who I would like to have on the other mediation, because the problem was not solved, and I told her Mr. Leonard Carlson, the new senior plant manager in charge. I left, to be called for another appointment on another day.

On October 1, 2001, I went to see my doctor, Dr. Denson. I took a work compensation form for him to fill out. I told him that I was nervous, because I was having problems at my job, and that a supervisor named Richard was harassing and threatening me, and the boss from the floor, when I told her, screamed and had a bad attitude toward me. My doctor diagnosed me with a stress reaction, exhaustion, anxiety, and emotional and mental trauma, all job-related.

On October 29, 2001, at approximately at 9:15, I left the working floor for my scheduled break. On my way to the machine, I told a coworker that I was going to the restroom, because I wasn't feeling well. Arnold told me that he was going to the men's room, and he would wait outside until I came out. I told him, "Thank you, Arnold."

While T was inside the restroom ready to come out, I heard Mr. Johnson page me. I came out of the restroom, and Arnold told me that Mr. Johnson was paging me. I told Arnold that I heard his page inside the restroom. We walked to the working floor, and I told Mohammed (204-B supervisor) that I had been in the restroom, because I wasn't feeling well, and Arnold was waiting for me. He said, "Okay," and we started working.

Mr. Johnson went to Arnold, and he gave him a 3971 for being late from break, and then he came to me and wanted me to sign a 3971 for being late from break. The form said that I was late by thirteen minutes. I told Mr. Johnson that I wasn't feeling well, and I had to go to the restroom, and that Arnold was worried and had waited for me.

November 7, 2001, Tina came to me and told me that I had to stay and work overtime. I told her that it was my day off the next day, and that I had an appointment early in the morning. On my days off, I made all my appointments, and that's why I could not stay. She told me that I could not leave. I went and got a PS 3971 form, filled out a "day off, doctor's appointment" request, gave it to Antoinette, and left.

But on November 21, 2001, Mr. Johnson called me to the conference room. When I got there with Bob, the shop steward, Mr. Johnson, told me that he was going to give me a notice of seven-days' suspension, signed by Mr. Johnson and ·Sonia, for *1) Unauthorized absence from your work area; and 2) failure to follow instructions.* I told Mr. Johnson that he knew why I was late from break on October 29, 2001, that I had submitted a number of medical reports to the doctor and nurse from the medical unit, and that all the supervisors knew about it. As for following instructions, sometimes I could not stay for overtime, because on my days off I made appointments for checkups with my doctor, and I had given management medical reports about that, too. I told him that I would like to know what management did with all those medical reports I had given them. After we finished talking, I went to the union office to file a grievance.

On November 23, 2001, I went to see my doctor, and I told him that I was having problems with management concerning overtime and going to the restroom. And he wrote me two letters to take to management.

I never got the fourteen days' suspension from Mr. Johnson.

On December 31, 2001, at approximately 8:27 p.m., I tried to give Tina a PS 3971 form. She looked at me and told me to give the form to Sonia. I asked her where she was, and she told me she was in the calling area. I went to look for Sonia. I gave Sonia the PS 3971, and she told me that no one was leaving. I looked at her, told her that I'd lost my best friend, and that I wanted to be with the family. Then I left Sonia with the 3971 form. I went back to my working area, and after two and a half hours, I ended my tour and went home.

I was off the next day, January 1, 2002.

On January 12, 2002, Tina called me to the conference room. I got a steward, and when I got there, she told me that the reason she had called me was for a notice of fourteen days' suspension, with the following charges: *Failure to follow instruction; AWOL.*

I went to the union office to file a grievance, stating everything that had happened on December 31, 2001 and January 1, 2002. I never got the fourteen-day suspension.

Don wrote a letter to the congressman, concerning the problem I was having with Richard and all of the suspensions that management was giving me.

The congressman wrote a letter to management, and he sent me a copy of management's response.

With all that had happened with Richard and the complaints from other coworkers, Sonia moved Richard to another location. After a year and a couple of months, on March 4, 2003, the COD and Appeal sent me a COD Investigation/ Affidavit to fill out. I didn't send it back, because Richard had been moved. I dismissed the complaint by not sending the affidavit. It took COD a year and six months to send me a letter.

Mr. Leonard Carlson, the plant manager, left, and Mr. Lawson stepped in and took over his position; Thomas Lawrence came back to work as a supervisor of the OCR machines.

One day, Sonia moved all the regulars to the machines, and all the flexes to the OCR machines. Because I was a flex, I was assigned to work on the OCR machines. Some employees told me that Thomas was going to be the supervisor on the OCR: I said, "Okay."

Another day, Sonia moved Thomas from the flat sorter machine to the OCR machines as a supervisor, I got a little scared, but I said to myself, *Let me see what could happen.* I always worked on machine number three with Lee, my partner.

One day, Thomas told me to go and work on machine number six that was located in front of the supervisor's desk. I went to the machine, where he told me to start working. I told Thomas that I would like Lee to be my partner, because she worked very well with me, and he said yes.

In the year 2003, Thomas looked at me a lot when I went to the work area. I started to work on machine number six, and while I was working, he came to my machine and started asking me questions, like, "If you get the flashing lights, what do you do?" I responded, "I go and clean the full stacker." And, "If you get a hard jam, what do you do?" I responded, "I go and take out the hard jam." After he asked me those questions, he told me that he was going to ask two more employees the same questions to see what they said, but I asked another female employee and she said to me that Thomas didn't ask her anything.

On May 6, 2003, I came to my work area and started working on machine number six on the sweep side. Cornelia, an assistant steward, came to my machine to talk to me. I was bending down, cleaning a stacker, and when I was going to put the tray of mail on the belt, Thomas was standing too close, behind me.

I froze, and said to him, "Excuse me?" He gave me a sexy smile. Thomas moved in front of Cornelia and me, and, looking at me, asked, "How do you say, 'You look good' in Spanish?" I didn't understand the question, because he had asked me the same question about four times. Cornelia asked him, "What is that question? That is sexual harassment!" I told Cornelia that it was in case he got a Spanish girlfriend. And Thomas looked at me and said, "I am going to the Dominican Republic." And he gave me another sexy smile.

I just moved quickly to the lower stackers and left them talking.

One day, I told my partner, Lee, what Thomas was doing to me, and she told me that a couple of times she had seen Thomas looking at my back in a naughty way.

On May 7, 2003, I was working on machine number six with Helen Rowland. We had finished the mail, and I went to talk to Rita about exercising.

Gloria Sanchez, who was working on the other machine next to Rita, came to join us in the conversation. Gloria's machine was running mail. Thomas came to the machine and told Gloria and me to go and collect the rejects from the machine. I told him, "Okay." But Thomas went to the rack and got the badges and came back to the machines, and in anger told me, "You! Go to the prime aisle and give Gloria and me the badge."

We went to the aisle, changed sort plant, then I went to the restroom, but when I came back to the aisle, Gloria was sent to the OCR. I saw Ms. Dorothy, the supervisor from the aisle, and I told her not to send me back to the OCR, because Thomas was acting up. She told me, "I don't need you here." And she called Mr. Johnson, and he told her to send me back to the OCR.

We went on our break at 9:45 p.m., and when we came back from break, the T-E "casual" was working on our machine. I saw the stackers full of mail, and I told the casual, "Please, sweep the stackers." He told me that the machine was full of mail when he had come to work on it. I told the casual that it wasn't true, because I was the one on the sweep side, and I had cleaned it before I left for my break. While I was talking with the casual, Thomas stared at me from a distance. I got nervous and went to load the ledge with mail.

When I was loading the ledge with mail, I turned around to get more mail from the belt, and found Thomas standing behind me, looking at me. I told him, "Thomas, please, next time tell the casuals to sweep the machine before they leave." Thomas got really angry and started screaming, "Amira, I want you in the back!" And I said to him, "*No*, why?" And he said, "You're not obeying; that is an order." But he never answered me as to why he wanted me in the conference room. Henry Miller was working next to my machine, and he said, "Amira, go." And I told Henry, "No." I got scared, because he was very angry.

He left, and I went the other way to look for Sonia. I saw Richard Rolle, an ex-steward, working on the machine, and I told him, "I want to talk to Sonia, now. Thomas is acting up again." Richard told me, "Amira, I am not supervising today. I don't have the walkie-talkie." Monica, who heard me say that to Richard, told me, "Amira, Sonia is in the ATAL."

I went to the ATAL window, and I told Sonia that Thomas had a bad attitude. Sonia told me, "Okay, I will talk to him." While I was talking to Sonia, Thomas came to the ATAL, and Sonia turned around and got really angry with him. Sonia mumbled to Thomas and moved her right arm really fast, and went to the corner where the desk was, to talk to Thomas. I left the ATAL window. I heard Doris paging me to go back to the NTAL room. I went to the ATAL, and I asked Doris who had asked her to page me. And she said she was just doing my job.

No one was there, just Doris, and I left. While I was walking away from the ATAL, there was another page.

It was Thomas: "Amira, come to the ATAL room." When I got there, I told him I needed a shop steward. I went and got Bob, and we went to the conference room. Thomas was there. We sat down on the chair and he (Thomas) told me that he was going to give me a Pre-Disciplinary Interview (PDI) for returning late from break. I told him that if I got a PDI, everyone else had to get one, too, because the crew had come at the same time. He told me that I had called him a pendejo, or "a sucker." I started to cry, and I told him he was lying, and I left the room, leaving the shop steward in the management conference room with him.

I left the room, because I knew that he was up to something, because I told Sonia about the way that he was acting with me. Minutes later, I saw Gloria hysterically crying, and she told me that Thomas gave her a PDI for coming in late from break. She said, "Amira, I took the supervisor test, and it's going to mess up my record for the position." Gloria told me that some of the coworkers were telling her that Thomas did that to her because she was working with me. I said to her, "Yes, I know." Gloria took Thomas to COD for harassing her. Her representative was Beth.

Sonia moved Gloria Sanchez to the flat sorter. And I was without a stable position at work.

One day, I was going to the flat sorter machine, and Sonia called me to the side. We sat down on the bench, and she asked me, "Amira, why haven't you said anything to him?" I told her, "How can I say something to him? He is the supervisor, and he has the power to do whatever he feels. When I talked to her, I was crying. And she asked me, "What do you want me to do? And I said, "Sonia, move him from here." She stood up, looked at me, and left.

LABOR RELATIONS

One night, at about 7:35 p.m., I was working on flat sorter machine number seven, and Sonia called me. She was with another woman. When I went to see what Sonia wanted me for, the woman: introduced herself to me as Ruth Weston from Labor Relations.

As we walked to Sonia's office, Mrs. Walton advised me that she was one of the investigators assigned to my complaint, and that the investigation would begin on Friday, May 23, 2003. I said to her, "Okay," and I left the office.

When I looked back, Mrs. Walton and Sonia were laughing. I just turned my face and started walking to my work area. While I was walking, I was thinking that I had seen the woman who had introduced herself to me in one of the personnel offices. I didn't trust anyone from the post office with my problem.

One morning, Don and I went for a walk, and he told me that he was going to buy me another house for my birthday. I got really happy, and Don stopped at a real estate office to see an advertisement about a four-family house they were selling. We went inside, and he did the paperwork. We talked to the real estate person, and we asked for the keys to see the house. I liked it, and we asked to hold the key from the house to do some fixing. Don, my son Rickuel, the handyman, and I fixed the house.

On May 9, 2003, I came to work, and Gloria and I looked for Mr. Johnson. We saw him, and I told him that I wasn't feeling safe, working for Thomas. Gloria told him about the harassment against her, and I told him that what Thomas was doing to me was sexual harassment. Mr. Johnson told us that he was going to talk to Sonia about the problem; he left, and I told Gloria, "Come with me to the union office. I want to talk to Beth."

When we got there, I told Beth that Thomas was acting up again, and Beth called Sonia, and told her that I was at the union office and we needed to talk to her. Sonia told Beth to meet her in the conference room. Gloria came to the conference room with us.

When Sonia came in, she sat on a chair, and I told Gloria to talk to Sonia first. Gloria told Sonia about Thomas harassing her. Sonia had a notebook, and she started writing down everything that Gloria said to her. When Gloria finished telling Sonia her problem with Thomas,

I told Sonia about the sexual harassment and harassment that Thomas did toward me on April 15, 2000. I told Sonia that Thomas started the sexual harassment when she changed him from the flat sorter machine to the OCR machine. A couple of times, he had come up behind me while I was waiting to begin my tour and whispered behind my shoulder, "You not saying hi to me tonight." Or he would come too close in front of me, saying, "You're not saying hello to me tonight." Or how Thomas would stand behind my back or come to my machine while I was working, just to look at me. Sonia said to me, in front of Gloria and the shop steward, that she was going to talk to him, and that she was going to move him in a moderate way, so that no one would know about the problem. She told me, Gloria Sanchez, and the union representative not to talk to anyone about this problem. We said, "Okay."

On May 10, 2003, I called the Complaint Organization Department, the COD, to file a complaint against Thomas.

On May 11, 2003, I was working in the aisle, sorting mail, and Thomas asked for me. He asked the 204-B supervisor, Mrs. Edith Smith, "Where is Amira?" Mrs. Smith told Thomas, "There she is." He came over to where I was working, looked at me, and smiled. I asked Thomas, "What are you looking at?" The Chinese woman who was working next to me asked, "What is wrong?" and I told her that Thomas was looking at me and smiling.

When Thomas left the working area, I went to Mrs. Smith and asked her for union time. I went to the union office and told Beth what Thomas was doing to me, stalking me, and making my life in the post office unbearable. I was scared and trembling, crying for help. But the union and management did nothing to stop him. I got home and I told Don, "I cannot take it anymore."

Don called the postal inspector from another facility on May 12, 2003. I was scared, because Thomas already had a history of sexual harassment, from the year 2000. I had filed a COD complaint against him. I cried to the inspector, "Please help me." The inspector gave me a number to talk to Inspector Adam Hall. I called M. Hall, and I told him what was going on, and that I was scared because this had been going on since the year 2000. He told me to file a COD complaint, and I told him I had filed a complaint. He told me to call him the next day.

The next day, I called him. He told me he had sent one of his inspectors to my facility, and the inspector spoke with the MDO from Tour-2. Mr. Hall told me to call him at any time if Thomas did something to me again (easier said than done).

On May 13, 2003, the Complaint Organization Department sent a package for me to fill out.

On May 18, 2003, Sonia assigned me to the flat sorter machine. On May 20, 2003, I sent the COD the form with my complaint.

On May 23, 2003, I received a call from Mrs. Walton. She told me that I was scheduled for an interview with her and a second investigator at 11:00 a.m. I told her that at that time I would be asleep. She told me that full consideration was given to the fact that Thursday was my scheduled day off, and a Friday morning appointment was not considered a burden. I told Mrs. Walton that I had my business, and I would like her to inform me first before she scheduled any appointments for the interview. She said to me that it was not management's intention to prolong the investigation, and that she would contact a second investigator and schedule for Friday, May 30, 2003.

On May 26, 2003, I was waiting to end my tour, and Thomas passed in front of me, staring at me in a way that made me uncomfortable.

On Tuesday, May 27, 2003, Sonia approached me to tell me that I was scheduled for an interview on May 30, 2003, at 11:00 a.m.

On Wednesday, May 28, 2003, I called Mrs. Walton and told her that I did not have enough notice for the interview to be scheduled on Friday, May 30, 2003. I asked Mrs. Walton why Sonia had to know about my interview, that she had my home phone number and my cellular number. I told her, "In the future, please notify me first." She informed me that she was required to inform the senior MDO for the Tour-3 about the scheduled changes for Tour-3 employees. She told me that Sonia would not be advised of the content of the meeting. I told her I wasn't sure if I would be able to attend the interview. She told me that I was aware that she was going to schedule the interview for Friday, and that the second investigator had revised his schedule to meet with me. She informed me that management had an obligation to investigate my complaint, so that they could try to resolve the issue. I said to her, "Yeah, Mrs. Walton told me that I needed to call her back by Thursday, May 29, 2003 to confirm the appointment for May 30, 2003, so that she could contact the second investigator." I told her that if I could not make it for the day of the interview, I would call her.

Friday, May 30, 2003, at about 9:50 a.m., Dori and I went to the facility and reported to the security officer on the first floor. The man from security contacted Mrs. Walton and told her that I was downstairs to see her. When she arrived on the first floor, she asked me what I was there for. I told her, "Because I have an appointment for the interview." She told me that on May 28, 2003, I had told her I wasn't sure if I could make the appointment. She then stated that I was supposed to have called her. She told me that she had cancelled my appointment. I told her that I was going to call her back if I could not make it for the interview. She told me she had called the second investigator and cancelled my appointment. It was after 10:00 a.m., and he would not be available on such short notice. She told me she would arrange another interview with the second investigator and me.

We went to her office, and she called the second investigator. She told me he was going to be available on Tuesday, June 3, 2003. I told her that I wanted Don present at the interview. Don told her he was not sure if he could make it for that day, because he needed to request the day off. She told me that I needed to call her by Monday, June 2, 2003, to confirm the appointment, and that she would be out of her office on Wednesday, June 4, 2003, until Friday, June 6, 2003. She informed me that management had no intention of prolonging the investigation. Don and I left her office and went to the union to talk to Benjamin. When we got to the union office, Benjamin was there, and I told him that Mrs. Walton from Labor Relations had cancelled my appointment. Benjamin told me that he was going to do an investigation.

The congressman wrote a letter to the postmaster and sent me a copy. I called Mrs. Walton and left her a message on her answering machine, stating that on June 9, 2003, I had sent her a fax and left her a message on her answering machine, making an appointment for June 14, 2003; but that was a Saturday, and I had meant June 13, 2003, Friday. I also said that she had never called me back to confirm the appointment, and if she had any questions, to call me."

On June 10, 2003, Mrs. Walton sent me certified mail for the interview. On June 11, 2003, I received a regular letter at home from Labor Relations for the appointment.

On June 12, 2003, I called the union president from Local Union-2, Mr. Abrams, but he was not in his office, and I spoke with William Cole, one of the shop stewards from Tour-2. I told him about the appointment with Labor Relations for June 13, 2003, and that I was going to cancel, because I was losing 1ny voice, and he told me that he was going to tell Benjamin. I called Mrs. Walton at about 2:30 p.m., and I left her a message on her answering machine, stating that l couldn't make it the next day because I was losing my voice, and if she had any questions, she needed to call me on my cellular phone. Then I went to the post office near where I live, to get a registered letter from Labor Relations.

On June 17, 2003, Richard Rolle, a 204-B supervisor, came running after me, three minutes before I began my tour, and he told me, "Amira, go to the OCR." I told Richard that I was supposed to report to my supervisor from the flat sorter first, and he told me, "No, the supervisor there is Thomas." I told him, "Okay, thank you."

After I clocked in, I went to the OCR and the supervisor told me to go to the prime aisle. So I went to the aisle to sort mail. Then I went to the machine, and who did I see there? Thomas, around my working area. I went to Shirley, my supervisor, and I asked her why Thomas was in my working area, and that I thought he was supposed to be supervising the flat sorter. She didn't answer me, she just looked at me, and I asked her for permission to take ten minutes off the working floor, because Thomas was around my working area, and she said, okay, go."

When I came back to the working area, Thomas was still around, and he was taking mail from the OCR machine. He was looking at me and smiling, like nothing was going on. "When management changed me to the flat sorter machine, he had orders not to be around my working area. I could not understand why, if Thomas was assigned to the flat sorter machine, he was on the OCR machine, picking up mail?

Senior Plant Manager Mr. Lawson wrote a letter to the congressman in response, and the congressman sent me a copy.

When I read the letter, I was hoping that the senior plant manager was going to do something about the sexual harassment against me.

On June 29, 2003, I began my tour at 6:30 p.m. I was assigned to work at the machine, but I had to go to the flat sorter because the same supervisor, Thomas, was assigned to supervise the OCR machines. I got upset, because management thought it was a game and didn't take what I was saying seriously. Every time I was assigned to work in another location, I had to be moved from there, because management from the work floor was moving Thomas to where I was assigned to work.

On July 3, 2003, I sent another fax to Mrs. Walton: *Mrs. Walton, call me at the number above to schedule an appointment with you and Mr. George Sand, as soon as possible.*

On July, 8, 2003, I was working on the flat sorter, and Sonia came to me and told me to go to the conference room. When I went inside the conference room, there was Mrs. Walton and a man, sitting and waiting for me. I looked at them, and I asked for permission to get a shop steward. I went to the ATAL room, and I asked the receptionist to call Bob, "the shop steward from the union."

The steward came to the ATAL room, and I told him that Labor Relations was in the conference room to interview me without giving me any notice. We went to the room, and they introduced themselves as Ruth Weston, from Labor Relations, and the man as an MDO, from another facility. The shop steward introduced himself as Bob, and he told them that he was not aware of the case. I told Mrs. Walton that I wasn't feeling well, and that I had left her a message about me losing my voice. Bob told them that I wasn't ready to go forward with the interview, and asked if they would reschedule the meeting. Mrs. Walton told the steward that I had made the complaint in May, 2003, and canceled the meeting three times. I told her that she had to understand that I could not force my voice. The shop steward told them I wasn't feeling well, and I was not prepared to go forward with the interview.

Mrs. Walton told the shop steward that she was aware that I had taken some days off because I was sick, and I had been back on full duty for several days. I was saying to myself, *What do my vocals have to do with my body?* I told her again that I was having problems talking, and she said that they would start the interview, and if I was having problems talking, we would take a break or stop the interview and continue on another day. The second investigator, the MDO for the other facility, started to explain management's role. I told him that Mr. Abrams, the union president, knew about my case, and that I wanted him present. Mrs. Walton told me that the interview was to allow me the opportunity to tell them what had happened, so that management could investigate the allegations. She told me that they weren't forcing me to talk, but I had filed a complaint with management and my congressman, and management was obligated to conduct an investigation. I was asked to give dates, and I told them that I did not have the information with me, and while I was talking, I felt pressure in my throat. At about 8:25 p.m., I told them that my throat was hurting. I stopped the interview for another day. Mrs. Walton told me that I was going to be notified of the next interview, and I needed to bring all my documentation or records.

On July 25, 2003, I began my tour, and when I began to work, Sonia came to my work area and told me that Mrs. Weston was in the conference room for the investigation. I left the work area, and when I got to the conference room, the second investigator and Mrs. Walton were there, waiting for me. I requested that I get Bob, my union representative, and I left the room to get him, but he was not at work. I saw another shop steward, "Diana," in the area, and I told her to go with me for the interview. She agreed, and we started walking to the conference room.

We got there and sat down, and Mrs. Walton asked me if I had the documentation that she had asked me for. I said yes, and I started the interview, pulled out my calendar, and gave them some of the dates when the supervisor had sexually harassed me. I provided copies of my 3971 form; the COD dated May 13, 2003, from my May 10, 2003, complaint; the date that I went to see the throat doctor; and all the names of the employees who had witnessed the supervisor doing the sexual harassment and harassing me. I told them that I had reported my sexual harassment to the Inspector's Service, and that my boyfriend had spoken with Inspector Adam, too. She asked me for the inspector's last name, but I did not remember, because I was too upset when I spoke to him. Mrs. Walton asked me to call her and give her the information, but I did not call her, because every time I talked about the problem I got sick.

In August of 2003, I went to work and started to look for a shop steward, and I saw Diana. I told her that I was going to Mrs. Walton's office to sign my statement, but I was not going to sign it because I did not tell them everything. About 7:20 p.m., I reported to the office of Labor Relations with the shop steward. When we got to the office, Mrs. Weston was waiting for me. She told me the reason I was there, and she gave me the statement to review and sign. I told her that I wanted to change my statement regarding a coworker, Gloria Sanchez, witnessing the bench incident, because it was not what I had told her in my interview on July 25, 2003. She corrected it in the computer, made a copy, and gave it to me to read. I agreed when I finished reviewing my statement, and she told me to sign it. I told her that I could not sign the statement, because I had not said everything. I asked her for a copy of my statement, and she told me that I was not getting one. I informed her that I could not sign it, and really quickly, while I was talking to her, with an attitude, she wrote, Refused to sign. She got a stamp, stamped really quickly, and told me that the post office was not keeping a copy of my statement. She took a lot of papers and shredded them. But meanwhile, everything I had said was written on the computer.

On October 3, 2003, COD sent me a letter, setting up my appointment for October 10, 2003. Before my appointment, Mrs. Jane cancelled the appointment, because she was going to take her vacation. But the reason she cancelled the appointment was because it was an investigation against Sonia. Sonia had told an employee that he was a homosexual, and that she was going to throw him out the balcony from the third floor; and Mrs. Jane was involved, for some reason. The employee got a lawyer, and for one reason or another, Sonia was escorted from the facility.

On December 15, 2003, I began my tour and went to my work floor, to the flat sorter; my supervisor, Mr. Douglas, sent me to work on the DBCS machine. I told him that I was not supposed to work around Thomas, and he told me that I wasn't going to work for him, that they needed me on the machine, and that I couldn't refuse. I told him that I wasn't refusing, and he said to me that the MDO, Mr. Green, told him to send me there.

I didn't say anything to him, and I walked to the DBCS area. The supervisor for that location was Trisha Anderson, who sent me to machine number three to work with Josephine Baker. I asked Josephine, "Do you want to feed, or do you want to sweep the machine?" She told me that she was going to sweep. I started feeding, and Thomas passed next to my machine and started to make faces, showing his teeth, and smiling. I told Josephine, and Josephine told me to ignore him. He passed in front of my machine a couple of times, making faces, and I got really nervous and called Josephine. I told her, "Josephine, he's harassing me in his own way." And I started to cry, and I said to Josephine, "You see him, and management doesn't do anything about it." I was crying and so nervous that Josephine took me to the restroom.

When we came back to the machine, Josephine told me that she was going to be on the feeding side. I told her okay, and she started feeding. I sat down on some trays, really low, so that Thomas wouldn't be able to see me. Josephine told me, "Amira, he's passing in front the machine, looking this way." I told Josephine, "I don't feel well, I think I have to go to the hospital after work. My chest is hurting me."

When I finished work at 12:30 a.m., I drove from the Winston facility to the hospital in Brooklyn and went to the emergency room. When I was called, I showed the nurse who called me that my left knee was swollen. He told me to put cream on it, and he sent me home. I got home at 4:40 a.m. and went to bed. When I woke up at 10:00 a.m., Don said to me, "Let's go to Tasty Donuts for hot chocolate." I said to him, "Okay, let me take a shower."

When I finished taking the shower, I went to my closet and took out my white shirt, my black and white skirt, put them on, got my high heels, and we left.

When we got there, I told Don that I wasn't feeling good, and we took the hot chocolate to go, and we came back home. I turned on the television, and I went and lay down on the leather sofa. Don started doing some business on the telephone. I stood up from the sofa and went to get a glass, to get some water, and my arm went to my chest like I was having a stroke. I could not move, and when Don looked at me, he asked, "You don't feel good?" I moved my right hand, telling him to hang up the telephone. Don grabbed me and walked me to the sofa. I could not walk or speak to him. When he sat me down, it got worse. My whole body went back, and then I got really scared and started fighting with whatever was happening to me. Don took the telephone and called for emergency services. I cried, and then my voice came back, and the only thing that I said was, "Oh my God, oh my God, please help me." I heard Don saying to me, "Don't worry, baby, I am here, I am here." While Don was talking on the telephone with the paramedics, I told him to put me on the floor. I wanted to move my body, because it was really stiff. He was so scared, seeing me like that, while he tried to help me. He did a good job.

The first ones who came to my rescue were the firemen. They gave me oxygen, and then the paramedic came and took me to the hospital. I was admitted to the hospital for seven days. Different doctors did a lot of tests, and they could not find anything. I left the hospital on December 23, 2004.

In January of 2004, I went back to work, and at 9:45 at night, after I returned from break, I started working on machine number eight on the flat sorter. Thomas passed between the machine and the wall; then looked at me and smiled.

On January 18, 2004, I went to the cafeteria and saw Thomas. When he saw me, he stood up from his chair, looking at me, grabbed the other chair in front of him, and pushed it with anger. I left the cafeteria.

When I started my tour and went to my working area, he was there, next to machine number eight, using the telephone. He looked at me and smiled. I went to my supervisor, Michael Douglas, and I asked him what he was doing in my working area. Michael told me that he was using the phone. I told him, "That's not the only telephone on the third floor," and I went to machine number seven and started working. Thomas left the area. On January 19, 2004, Thomas came to my work area at 6:20 p.m., smiling, with a shop steward.

On February 8, 2004, I could not find my badge to begin my tour, so I went to the prime aisle and asked Mrs. Smith, who was supervising on the OCR (Mrs. Jane was there), and she answered my question. Thomas asked, *"Why? I didn't say anything."* I just turned around and left for the flat sorter machine.

On February 9, 2004, I started working on the OCR with a lady named Pat on machine number two. I was on the sweep side, and Thomas came to the end of the machine and started talking with an employee named Anton. He talked to him for almost twenty minutes, and then he left.

At 8:25 p.m., I told Pat that it was time for lunch, and I left. I went to the cafeteria and got a green tea, because I couldn't eat, and while I was drinking my tea I started thinking that Mr. Green had told me Thomas wasn't going to be around my working area.

I finished my tea, and at about 8.55 p.m., I started walking to my working area. When I came back to the machine, I started working on the feeder side, but I was working so fast that I had to stop feeding the mail at 11.25 p.m., and I went to help Pat because the stackers were full of mail.

At 11:32 p.m., Thomas crossed the area and passed next to machine number two. When I finished helping Pat sweep the stackers, I went to the feeding side, and I saw him. I turned back and went to Pat, and told her, "He is here." She said to me, "He is not supposed to be here." Thomas came and started talking to Richard Rolle, my supervisor.

When Thomas left, I went to my supervisor and told him that Thomas was not supposed to be around my working area. He told me to talk to the MDO in charge. I told him I was going to take a few minutes off the working floor, and he told me okay.

I went to the restroom, and one of my friends came in and asked me, "Are you okay?" I told her what had happened, and she said to me, "Amira, these people don't care about anything." I told her, "I know."

On February 16, 2004, the supervisor from the flat sorter didn't needed me, and he sent me to work in the prime aisle, sorting mail. Thomas came to the manual aisle, went to an employee named Henry Miller, and started to scream at him. Every employee who was working on the aisle stopped working and looked at what was going on with Henry Miller.

One day, Henry Miller came to me and asked me to write a letter for him, stating what I saw on the day that Thomas came to the manual aisle and started screaming at him. I wrote the letter for him.

MARCH 12, 2004

To Whom It May Concern:

My name is Amira, Tour-3 Clerk. I am writing this letter on behalf of Henry Miller. Henry Miller has been a victim of Mr. Lawrence.

SEXUAL HARASSMENT IN THE POST OFFICE

On February 16, 2004, I witnessed Mr. Lawrence screaming in Henry Miller's face, on the manual aisle. Mr. Lawrence was very unprofessional toward Henry Miller.

Mr. Lawrence has a history of sexual harassment (I've been a victim and talking to employees in a hostile manner.

Sincerely,
Amira

On April 6, 2004, I came to work at 6:40 p.m. Supervisor Michael Douglas wanted me to go to the prime aisle. I told Michael not to send me to the aisle, because I had chest pain, due to Thomas, and he said, "That is not my problem, go and talk to someone." Madeline Bradbury heard me talking to Mr. Douglas, and she said, "I'll go to the aisle." I told Madeline, "Thank you."

On May 16, 2004, I began my tour, starting to work on the flat sorter machine, and the supervisor from the flat sent me to the prime aisle. I started working on aisle 043, sorting mail in the cases. I was working next to my friend, Pito.

Thomas came to the working area and passed between a u-car and me, so closely behind my back that he rubbed the right side of his body against my back. I jumped off my seat quickly, and went to the other side of aisle 033. Thomas went to get the casuals, and they went around the aisle. Thomas looked at me and gave me a happy smile. I got more scared, and went back to the other side of the aisle where I was working. I moved the u-car and sat down, shaking. I asked Pito, "Did you see that?" And he said, "No, I was sorting mail."

Some employees saw me jumping out of my seat, and they started talking about it. Minutes later, Thomas used the pager to start calling more casuals, and at 8:04 p.m., he paged another employee.

On May 24, 2004, Thomas came to the flat sorter for ten minutes to use the phone. All the workers saw him and stared at him as he smiled.

Don wrote a letter to the senior plant manager, Mr. Lawson, on May 25, 2004. He sent him the letter, because we didn't hear anything about the complaint that I had made, and I saw the supervisor doing the same thing every day to the employees and to me.

Mr. Lawson,

My name is Don, the husband of Amira. I spoke to you not so long ago, on the phone, about Mr. Lawrence's sexual harassment of Amira. I was hoping you could give me an update on her case. Ruth Weston from Labor Relations did not keep us informed. It seems like it was swept under the rug. Not too long ago, in the month of April, 2004, I received a call from Amira. She seemed very upset, and her voice was trembling. She stated that her MDO, Mr. Green, was forcing her to work in the same area as Mr. Lawrence. I told Amira that I would like to speak to Mr. Green. Mr. Green told me that Amira was overreacting, and that if she did not follow his instructions, he would have to give her a disciplinary action. This has been going on since the year 2000. What is the post office doing, or what are you doing? This is a very serious matter. There is no reason why a postal employee, who is a good worker, has to come to the work floor and not feel safe.

Don

On May 25, 2004, I began my tour at 6:20 p.m. I went to my working area, the flat sorter, and Thomas was there, sitting in front of the computer, talking to Sarah Banks. I turned back and went around machine number eight. I saw Henry Miller, and he told me, "Thomas is here." I told him, "I know."

At 9:30 p.m., I went to take my break. I saw Cornelia, and I told her that I had chest pains, and that the pain had started when I saw Thomas in my working area. We talked for a little while, and she left.

When I finished my break at 9:45 p.m., I went back to my working area, and Thomas was at my working area again. I went around the machine again, and Henry saw me and told me, "Thomas is here again." I told him, "I know." I went to the other side of the machine, where I was supposed to be working. I went to get something in my bag, and Thomas looked at me and smiled. I got really scared, because I knew Thomas was harassing me in his own way, and my eyes got watery. Henry saw me, and he called me to the other side of the machine, where he was working, and Henry said to me, "Don't get like that. That's what he wants." I told Henry, "I cannot help it." I told Henry I wasn't feeling well, and he told me to go to the nurse. He asked me, "Do you want me to call Shirley, the supervisor?" I told him, "Yes, call her."

Shirley came to the machine, and I told her that I wasn't feeling well, and I needed to see the nurse. Shirley went to get the medical form, and she took me to the medical unit. I told the nurse that my chest was hurting me. I was crying, and I told her that it was because of Thomas. The nurse told me that she couldn't do anything about it, and to talk to management. I told her that management wasn't doing anything about it. I told her that I had left my medication, nitro, at home, and to please send me home. She said to me that it was up to management to make that decision. I told the nurse, "Okay." My eyes were really red, because when I was talking to the nurse, telling her my problem, I was crying. Then the nurse gave me a copy of the medical form, and she told Shirley that I wanted to go home because I had left my medication at home. Shirley called Mr. Green, and told me that I had to make an accident report. I told her that I was too sick to make a report, and they called the union representative, Janet Brooks.

When I saw her, I told her that I had severe chest pains, and that I wanted to go home because I had left my medication at home. Janet called someone at the union office, and they told her that I needed to go to the hospital. Then Janet told me that we had to go to the conference room.

When we got to the room, Shirley had a lot of papers from the DA-1 form. I was crying, because the pain was too much. Shirley told Janet that I had to file an accident report. I told them that I was in too much pain to be answering questions or filling out forms, and that I wanted to go to the hospital.

Mr. Green came to the conference room and asked me, "Amira, do you want to go to the hospital?" I told him, "Yes, I don't feel good." And Mr. Green called the ambulance. While waiting for the paramedics, Shirley gave me the form to fill out. I told her, crying, that I was in pain, but I ended up filling out some of the questions, like my name and the cause of the pain. The paramedics came to the conference room, and I told them that I was having bad pain in my chest. They took me to the ambulance, took blood, and gave me aspirin and nitro. Then my chest pain got a little better. They took me to the emergency room, and I cried and told the doctor what had happened. She asked me, "Why didn't they do something about it?" I told her, "I don't know."

A couple of hours later, I was released. I went to my doctor for a follow-up, and he cleared me to return to work on June 1, 2004.

Don was so stressed out from the things that were going on, and how no one was doing anything about it. He wrote a letter to everyone else to help me:

On May 25, 2004, my wife, Amira, had a problem with Supervisor Lawrence. It was job-related. Amira had severe chest pain, which she gets under severe stress. She then proceeded to go to the medical unit to see the nurse, because she had no medication. She takes nitroglycerin under her tongue for her chest pains. Amira told the nurse that she wanted to go home. The nurse refused to send Amira home. She told Amira that it was up to management to send her home. In a medical situation, it is up to the medical unit, not management, to send her home. It seems to me that, because it was job-related, and Mr. Lawrence is to blame, they were giving Amira a hard time. Amira requested to be taken to the hospital. If she had not requested to go to the hospital, with the nurse telling her she could not go home, who knows what damage she could have endured? The pain and suffering that she has to go through is a disgrace. The post office and management are fully responsible.

Sincerely,
Don

On May 28, 2004, I went to work in the morning to speak with Benjamin, but he was not at the facility, and so I asked for Shop Steward William Cole. I told William my problem, and we went upstairs to talk with Mr. Lawson. But the one who called us was Mr. Green.

Mr. Green took us to his office, and I told Green my problem again, but it was like I was talking to a wall. Mr. Green took out a DA-16, a form for the workers' comp board.

Mr. Green filled it out, went out of his office, and came back with Plant Manager Mr. Lawson and some papers from FMLA that my doctor had filled out. Mr. Green asked me, "Who was the person that filled out the forms?" I told him that the one who had filled them out was my doctor. Mr. Lawson told me, in front of the steward, that he was going to take care of the problem.

Then we left the office. Mr. Cole told me that he was going to talk to Benjamin about the conversation in the office.

On May 31, 2004, Don wrote another letter to the senior plant manager, because he didn't get any response from the first letter:

I spoke to you on the telephone a few times about Supervisor Lawrence and his sexual harassment of my wife, Amira. I was hoping that you could give me an update on her case. Ruth Weston, of Labor Relations, did not keep us informed. It seems like she swept it under the rug. Not so long ago, in the month of April, 2004, I received a call from my wife. Amira seemed very upset, and her voice was trembling. MDO Green was forcing her to work in the same area as Mr. Lawrence. I told Amira that I would like to talk to Mr. Green. Mr. Green told me that my wife was overreacting. If it was his wife who had been sexually harassed by Mr. Lawrence from the year 2000, and management had done nothing about it, how would he feel? Mr. Green also said that if Amira did not follow instructions, he would have to give her a disciplinary action. He also told me that he would escort her to the area where Mr. Lawrence was working. Now you're telling me that Amira needs a bodyguard?

This is a serious matter. There is no reason a postal employee, who is a good worker, has to come to the work floor and not feel safe.

Sincerely,
Don

Benjamin called me to tell me that he had made an appointment with the plant manager for me to talk to him. I told Don, and he told me that he was going to go with me, because he wanted to know what was going on.

On June 1, 2004, I went to work and gave my doctor's notes to Mr. Green. He told me that I couldn't work, and sent me home.

On June 2, 2004, Don and I went to the union office, early in the morning. I told Benjamin all of the things that Thomas was doing to me, and how no one was doing anything about it.

We went upstairs to the conference room to talk to Senior Plant Manager Mr. Lawson. I started the conversation by telling him that Thomas had been doing this since the year 2000, and he had started doing it again, always when I was by myself, and to other females. I told him that he was a wise guy. Mr. Geer told me, in front of the union president, and another manager, that there was another female employee who had made a complaint of sexual harassment against him. But they had done an investigation, and it was at a club where they had had a couple of drinks, and that nothing had happened. Don told him, "Can all the women who complained be wrong?" Mr. Lawson didn't answer Don's question, and he looked at me and gave me two options: He could transfer me to another facility, or I could go to the midnight tour. I asked him, "Why do I have to be the one to be removed? I wasn't the one causing trouble." He told me that Thomas had his rights. And I said to him, "And I have my rights, too." Then I told Don, "I think that we wasted our time coming here."

And we stood up, and we left. We went to the union office with Benjamin, and · I told him that Mr. Green had sent me home after reading my doctor's notes. Benjamin went to the file cabinet, and he took out the grievance form and gave it to me to fill out, and I started writing: *On June 1, 2004, I came to work, being cleared by my doctor to come back to work full time. I gave Mr. Green all of my paperwork, and he told me I couldn't work, then he sent me back home. Mr. Green is not a doctor. If I was cleared by my doctor, I should have been able to work.*

I received a letter, dated June 2, 2004, stating that I was to return for work. Management made the decision to change me to another tour, so I would not have to be around Supervisor Lawrence.

On Friday, June 3, 2004, I left my home at 10:30 p.m., and got to the post office at 11:30 p.m. I went to the cafeteria and sat down with my friends from Tour-3 until 11:55 p.m., and then went to the ATAL room to get my badge.

I asked the receptionist from Tour-1 to page Cynthia Lee, the MDO, because I was assigned to work on Tour-1, and she was going to assign me to my working area. Ms. Lee came to the ATAL and told me that I was assigned to work on flat sorter 100. She escorted me to my working area. I stood next to machine number seven, and I didn't move from there. I was looking at the crew from flat sorter 100 going to the machines to work.

The supervisor from flat sorter 100, Steve Parker, came to me, and said, "Amira, you can go to any machine on this tour. No one is assigned to any machine." I said to myself, Oh my God, because when I came from Tour-3, I was assigned to work on just one machine, unless someone was off or absent, and then I was told to go and work on another machine. I told the supervisor that I was working on machine number seven on Tour-3, and I really didn't want to run all over the machines, and he told me okay, but I didn't have to. And I went to work on machine number seven. I was really sad, asking myself every minute, *What did I do wrong?* But, every night, my friends from Tour-3 came to see me at the flat sorter to see how I was doing. One morning, I went to the post office to talk to Benjamin Abrams, and I made another grievance: *It is a disgrace, what Plant Manager Mr. Lawson and his crew, MDO Mr. Green, MDO Jane, Supervisor Sarah Banks, and the shop steward, have done to me. I am being punished for coming forward about Supervisor Lawrence's sexual harassment, and I'm being put on the midnight tour.*

I am the victim. I spoke to Plant Manager Mr. Lawson about Mr. Lawrence, and my husband spoke to him about a year ago on the phone, too. Why didn't they listen to me?

This also refers to MDO Sonia. I went to her crying and begging, and she did nothing. I want to go back to Tour-3. I am not happy on Tour-1.

I will not stop until I get some kind of satisfaction.

I received a letter, dated June 7, 2004, from the Employee Standards Association Office. They were asking me for additional information in order to make a determination regarding my claim. They advised me to respond within thirty days or my claim may be denied.

With the questionnaire, I sent them one of the letters that Don had written to the plant mana May 25, 2005.

On June 9, 2004, I received a letter from the Employee Standards Association Office, stating that my claim was insufficient to establish that I had sustained an injury on May 25, 2004. If I had received any medical treatment from a physician, clinic, or hospital for an injury, I should arrange for submission of the medical records. Since I identified, in addition to chest pains, stress, a physician's report from a psychiatrist or clinical psychologist had to be submitted that included: *Dates of examination and treatment; history of injury given by the physician; detailed description of findings; results of all x-rqys and laboratory that followed; diagnosis and clinical course of treatment that followed; and the physician's opinion supported by a medical explanation as to how the reported work incident caused or aggravated the claimed injury. This explanation was crucial to my claim.*

I went to work, began my tour at 12:00 a.m., and when I went to my work area, Supervisor Sarah Banks told me that she had to talk to me. I asked Tyron, the shop steward from my work area, to go with me, and when we went to the conference room, Shirley was there with MDO Green.

Shirley told me that the reason she had called me was that I had a problem with my work performance, and I needed help. She recommended I to go to the EPA program. I told Shirley that I didn't need to go to EPA. I told Shirley that the person who had the problem was Thomas. I reminded her of the night that I was in the cafeteria and Thomas raised his hands at me like he was going to hit me. I told her, "You came in and saw him when he hit the wall, and saw me trembling like he was going to hit me." Shirley didn't comment when I told her that. She gave me the letter, I looked at them, and I left the conference room, went to my working area, and started to work.

I ended my tour at 6.00 a.m., and when I got home I took the letter out of the envelope and started to read the letter from the Referral to the Environmental Protection Agency (EPA).

When I finished reading the letter, I got upset, because she knew what was going on, and she was acting like she didn't know anything.

The next day, in the afternoon, while I was doing some work on the computer, my friend Lou, who worked as a carrier in Puerto Rico, signed in online. I sent him an instant message. I told him that nobody was doing anything about my problem with Thomas, and he was doing the same thing all over to other women. He told me, "Amira, write a letter to Andy Whitehorn, because Mr. Whitehorn doesn't like sexual harassment." I told him, "Okay, I will write him a letter." And when I finished talking to him, I wrote the letter to Mr. Whitehorn, stating:

SEXUAL HARASSMENT IN THE POST OFFICE

Dear Mr. Whitehorn,

I need to see you. I have a very serious problem. My name is Amira. I work as a mail processor. Mr. Lawson is the plant manager. My husband spoke with Mr. Lawson on the telephone a year ago about my problem with Mr. Lawrence.

In the year 2000, I took Supervisor Lawrence to the COD for sexual harassment, and he wrote me an apology letter.

I have spoken to Mr. Lawson about Supervisor Lawrence and his sexual harassment. Everyone seems to be protecting him, including, just mentioning a few, MDO Jane, MDO Green, SDO Sarah Banks, Local-2 Steward Mrs. Brooks, and Plant Manager Mr. Lawson. This has been going on since the year 2000. What a disgrace. How can something like this go on so long? This is something so serious, and management has turned their backs.

In the year 2003, I went to MDO Sonia, crying and begging her to help me with the problem of Mr. Lawrence. She laughed and did nothing. She could have stopped it, but she thought it was a big joke. Some joke. I even wrote a letter to my congressman.

Now on July 2, 2004, MDO Green sent me a letter that my Tour-3 has been changed to Tour-1. Mr. Whitehorn, why am I being punished for coming forward about Mr. Lawrence? I have gotten sick over this, with severe chest pains, and I had to make an appointment to see a psychiatrist. I tried everything, hoping that management would take care of this problem.

Please, Mr. Whitehorn, I need your help.

Sincerely,
Amira

One afternoon, Don told me that he was going to send the same letter that he had sent Mr. Lawson (five months ago) to the injury board. He started to look for the letter, found it, went to the copy machine, made a copy, and he said to me, "This is the letter," and started to read it to me:

My wife, Amira, had a problem with Supervisor Lawrence. It was job-related. Amira had severe chest pain, which she gets under severe stress. She then proceeded to go to the medical unit to see the nurse, because she had no medication. She takes nitroglycerin under her tongue for her chest pains. Amira told the nurse that she wanted to go home. The nurse refused to send Amira home. She told Amira that it was up to management to send her home.

In a medical situation, it is up to the medical unit, not management, to send her home. It seems to me, because it was job-related, and Mr. Lawrence is to blame, they were giving Amira a hard time. Amira requested to be taken to the hospital. If she did not request to go to the hospital, with the nurse telling her she could not go home, who knows what damage she could have endured. The pain and suffering that she has had to go through is a disgrace. The postal office and management are fully responsible.

When he finished reading the letter, I just looked at him and didn't say anything. I was thinking about the bad pain that I had had that day, and how no one had helped me in that moment. He got an envelope, put the letter inside, sealed it, got a stamp from the shelf, and told me, "I'll be right back; I am going to the mailbox to send this letter." I said to him, "Okay," and he left.

Two days later, I wrote a letter in response to Sarah.

To Sarah Banks:

The reason for this letter is because you gave me an assistance referral to the Environmental Protection Agenry (EPA) on June 09, 2004.

All of a sudden, you are concerned about me going to EPA. What a joke. Now that I am on Tour-1, it doesn't make any sense. When I was on Tour-3, you never questioned my work performance.

You are trying to state that I have a problem? Yes, I do have a problem: you not coming forward about what you witnessed in the cafeteria when Supervisor Lawrence raised his hands toward me, slapping the wall, and me trembling, thinking that he was going to hit me.

You are the one who needs to go to EPA, with the rest of management, who are covering for Supervisor Lawrence.

Sincerely,
Amira

On July 6, 2004, I wrote a letter to the congressman, because I was seeking help inside the post office, and they had just turned their backs on me.

Mr. Congressman:

My name is Amira. I have worked at the post office in New York for six years. The plant manager is Mr. Lawson. I've been sexually and verbally harassed by my sttpervisor, Mr. Lawrence, since the year 2000. My hours were from 7:00 p.m., to 12:30 p.m. For the past five years, I have been on Tour-3. Mr. Lawson changed my tour from 12:00 a.m. to 6:00 a.m. Why I am being moved? I am the victim. Move Supervisor Lawrence. I want to go back to my regular working hours. Management has done nothing to solve the problem.

I am not the only one being sexually harassed or harassed by the same supervisor. Please help us.

Sincerely,
Amira

LETTERS OF COMPLAINT AGAINST MR. LAWRENCE

One afternoon, I called the union office and Benjamin answered the telephone, I told him that I was looking for statements from workers who had been sexual harassed and harassed by Thomas, and I asked him to write a statement for me. He told me that he was going to write it, and he would fax it to me the next day. I told him, "Thank you, I'll talk to you later, because I have to make a few calls." He said, "Okay, Amira," and I hung up the telephone to call Geoffrey, to also ask him for a statement. When Geoffrey answered the telephone, I told him who I was, and he said, "What's up, Amira?" I told him that I was calling him to see if he could write a statement for me concerning Thomas, and he said: "Sure I will, tomorrow I'll have it for you." I told him that I appreciated all the things that he was doing for me, and I thanked him for his help. He said, come to the office tomorrow, to get the statement. I said, "Okay, bye," then I called Henry and I asked him to write a statement for me, because he was having problems with Thomas, too, and he said, "I will write the statement for you, look for me tomorrow," and I asked him if he could help me get a statement from the employees who had problems with Thomas. He told me that coworkers had written statements against Thomas before, and that he would get them for me, and that he was going to help me in every way, because Thomas was doing the same thing all over again. He said to me that Shaquinta was also having problems with him, and no one was doing anything about it. He said, "Amira, go and talk to her to see if she will write a statement for you." I told him, "I will talk to her tomorrow," and I left because it was time for me to begin my tour.

The next day, when I woke up, I looked at my fax machine and I had one fax. When I looked at it, it was Benjamin's statement.

When Don came home from work at 5:30 p.m., I showed him the statement and he started to read it; he said, "Why is management not doing the right thing?" I said, "I don't know" He said, "Anyway, get ready. Let's go out and eat dinner." I told him, "Let me take a shower, real quick."

I got dressed and we left. He took me to DD's restaurant, I asked for my wine, and salmon with vegetables. Don ordered his pasta like always. When we finished eating, we came home and I went to sleep.

The next day, I went to work and straight to the union office, and Geoffrey was there, waiting for me. He gave me the statement and I told him that I was going upstairs to see Henry, because he was helping me get statements. I thanked him again for his help, and he said, "You're welcome, Amira," and I left the office.

I went to the flat sorter, where Henry was working. I said, "Hi, Henry," and he said, "I got the statements for you." He told me to wait, that he was going to get the statements. He came back and gave them to me. I told him, "Thank you, Henry, I owe you one; talk to you later," and I left because he was working.

Henry asked one of the employees if I could get the letter that she had written about Thomas in April. She said okay, and gave it to me.

On July 19, 2004, I went to my doctor because I was weak, stressed, and losing weight too fast in the forty-five days that I was in tour one. He gave me a letter to take to management, but I didn't give them the letter because I was worried about my job. Management didn't like it when I came forward against Thomas. What I did was keep the letter and wait to see if I could get better. Every night that I went to work, I felt very weak.

AUGUST 13, 2004

One night, I wasn't feeling well, but I went to work. When I got to the work floor, I felt like I was going to faint, and I said to myself, It is time to go. *While going to my work floor, I was looking for an MDO, and I saw Jessica*

Hud. I called her and told her that I wasn't going to keep working. She started to walk very quickly, and she said I had to go to the flat sorter. I was so weak that I could not talk or walk. I followed her to the flat sorter machine, and she asked the supervisor, "Where is Amira's badge?" The MDO was acting like she was ignoring me when I was trying to talk to her. I called Jessica to the side, and I told her that it was an emergency. I was feeling weak, and I was losing weight too quickly. I told Jessica, "I am not staying." I gave her the letter that my doctor gave me on July 19, 2004. Jessica told me to get a 3971 Form, and I told her that I was too weak to go and get the form and bring it back to her. I said to her, "Please, Jessica, I feel really sick." And she told me that she was going to fill out the 3971 for me. I told her, "Thank you," and left without beginning or ending the tour. The letter I gave to Jessica stated:

JULY 19, 2004

Feels weak, stressed, anxious, has episodes where she is frightened about her health. Weight has gone up to 135 pounds early this month, and has fallen since to 127 pounds. Appetite is poor. Has chest pressure on moderate exertion. Chest wall syndrome continues. Has anxiety state, anorexia. PRIOR Myositis, tendonitis. HO kidney stones. Hx of stress reaction with exhaustion, anxiety state, with emotional upset and mental trauma, job related. Has been advised that she is to be started on a night shift. She is anxious about this change and the effect that this will have on her. Her condition has become worse since her notification of the shift change. I strongly advise against the shift change. Return in two weeks.

One day, I was thinking of the times that I had seen Thomas standing in front of the door while I was going to begin my tour, and I wrote a letter to the senior plant manager.

AUGUST 16, 2004

To Mr. Lawson:
Mr. Lawson, you told me that you changed my tour so that Supervisor Lawrence would not harass me. Then tell me, why is it that Mr. Lawrence is standing at the front of the floor at the time that I have to report to work.
August 4, 2004, I saw Mr. Lawrence at 11:45 p.m. in front of the third-floor door with MDO Green.

August 5, 2004, when I came out of the elevator Mr. Lawrence was standing in front of the door at 11:53 p.m. and I had to go to the cafeteria.

August 6, 2004 at 11:45 p.m., I came out the cafeteria and I went through the third-floor door and Mr. Lawrence was standing there.

Mr. Lawson, Supervisor Lawrence is stalking me.

Respectfully,
Amira
Mail Processor

On August 17, 2004 I received a letter from Ms. Lee, manager of distribution operations. She enclosed an Employee Work Limitation Form, to be filled out by my doctor. She also requested that I submit medical documentation for my request.

I wrote a letter to Cornelia, one of my witnesses.

AUGUST 18, 2004

To Mrs. Cornelia:

On June 16, 2004, I asked you to write a letter disclosing the sexual harassment of Mr. Lawrence. You replied, "Amira, you are going to get me in trouble." I told you that you would not get in trouble, and you told me that, "Mr. Lawrence does the same thing to you." But you never said whether or not you were going to write the letter for me.

On June 25, 2004, I approached you again to write the letter for me, and you said, "I cannot remember." How can you not remember, when Mr. Lawrence was so close to me, when I was bent down putting mail in the tray, and I turned around and said to him, "Excuse me?" and he asked me, in front of you, "How do you say, 'You look good' in Spanish?" And with a serious voice, you told him, "What is that question? That is sexual harassment." At the time you were an assistant steward, Cornelia. You cannot hide something like that. You know that Mr. Lawrence sexually harasses almost all the women from the facility.

Respectfulfy,
Amira

SEXUAL HARASSMENT IN THE POST OFFICE

The registered nurse from the medical unit sent me a letter with a procedural reissue on the subject of light-duty assignments, and a letter signed by Dr. Perkins with a lightduty form dated August 17, 2004, to take to my doctor.

It was stated that the documentation submitted, though somewhat informative, did not provide them with adequate details or the medical information needed to make the proper recommendation to management.

In order for them to properly finalize approval for Work Return Medical recommendation, the following information was still needed:

They requested that I complete the Medical Information Request form, as well as the Physical Work Limitation form, on the reverse of the request. An adequate response to both (front and reverse sides) was still needed.

I took the work limitation form to my doctor, he filled it out, and I sent it back to management with a letter of my diagnoses.

On August 18, 2004, I received another certified letter from management. I was advised that my medical restrictions could not be evaluated or approved until I submitted the complete medical documentation requested by Dr. Perkins, postal officer. As such, I was not permitted to return to work until my medical restrictions and physical limitations were properly evaluated by the postal medical officer.

I was advised that any request for continuation of light duty beyond thirty days must be submitted in writing to the senior plant manager, together with an updated work limitation form, no later than seven days prior to the expiration of the current light duty assignment. Then a review of that documentation would determine my continued duty stat us. Failure to follow the procedures could result in a delay processing the request for a light-duty assignment, or termination of a light-duty assignment.

The RN from the medical unit was giving me a hard time about making an appointment with the Postal Medical Officer, so Don wrote a letter to him and to my primary doctor, to see if doctor-to-doctor contact could get me back to work.

The following are letters that I faxed to the doctor from the rnedical unit and my doctor.

To Dr. Perkins:
 This letter is on behalf of Amira. Please get in contact with her physician, Dr. Denson.

Sincerely,
Don

AUGUST 18, 2004

To Dr. Denson:
 Please get in touch with Dr. Perkins, medical unit at the post office. Maybe doctor-to-doctor, you can get Amira back on the day tour.

Sincerely,
Don

On August 20, 2004, I filed a grievance to see the doctor from the medical unit, and faxed it to the president of the union, Benjamin Abrams.

To: Benjamin Abrams
 I need to see Dr. Perkins at the medical unit; it is a medical emergency. I have tried a number of times to make an appointment to see Dr. Perkins. For some reason, the medical unit is preventing me from seeing Dr. Perkins.

Yours Truly,
Amira

In the month of August, I received a letter from the congressman, which he sent to the postmaster general.
 I filed another grievance and faxed it to Benjamin Abrams:

Benjamin Abrams, I need to see the doctor at the medical unit. It is a medical emergency. I tried a number of times to make an appointment to see him, and for some reason, the medical unit nurse is preventing me from seeing Dr. Perkins in person.

I received a certified letter from management, and I faxed it to Benjamin Abrams.

On August 26, 2004 I sent Mr. Lawson some paperwork, and wrote a letter to the medical doctor.

To: Senior Plant Manager,
I am sending you the employee work limitation form and my physician's letters.

Respecfully,
Amira
Mail Processor

Dear Dr. Perkins:
My name is Amira. I was working on Tour-3. I made a complaint to management about a supervisor and his sexual harassment of me, and management changed me to Tour-1. Since they changed me to the night shift, my condition has become worse, and I am scared about my health. The night shift is killing me. I have been out of work since August 13, 2004. Dr. Perkins, please help me.

Sincerely,
Amira

Attached Dr. Denson's letter and the medical information form that the RN from the medical unit sent me.

Management sent me a certified letter, regarding my work status, a request for additional medical documentation, and a light-duty form from the medical office.

I faxed the letter that management sent me to Benjamin. Management was sending me the forms for my doctor to fill out almost every two days.

On August 30, 2004, I received another certified letter. When I opened it, it was the medical documentation, lightduty assignments, and an employee work-limitation form, to take to my doctor.

In the afternoon, I filed another grievance and faxed it to Benjamin on September 1, 2004: *I've been out of work sick since August 13, 2004. I request* that I go back to work on light duty, and Plant Manager Mr. Lawson has denied me. My doctor gave me a medical letter, requesting to change my tour, be put on light duty, and to go back to work immediately, and management is not letting me go back to work.

I was out of work for eighteen days because management is denying me from going on light duty.

I wrote a letter to the senior plant manager.

AUGUST 31, 2004

Mr. Lawson:

There is no reason for you to retaliate against me. How could you deny me light duty when the medical unit is preventing me from seeing Dr. Perkins. I am sick and I will go on light duty, because you have people on light duty picking their noses and doing nothing, and I have been on light duty for years.

I will like to know why you and management are protecting Thomas Lawrence.

Respectfully,
Amira

Management was sending me the forms, day after day. I faxed twelve pages that management sent me to the union president.

One night, I was doing some work on my computer, and I decided to look at my email. One of my friends from the job sent me an email.

On September 7, 2004 I went to see my psychiatrist, and she wrote me a letter to take to management.

I faxed Benjamin Abrams the diagnoses from my doctors, which I sent to management, and the letter asking to return to work.

On September 8, 2004, I wrote a letter to Benjamin, because Mr. Lawson was denying my light duty.

To Benjamin Abrams:

My doctor has cleared me to go back to work on light duty as soon as possible, "immediately."

Mr. Lawson and management are stating that there is no work for me on light duty. This is absolutely a case of retaliation and discrimination against me.

There are many people of all races and colors on light duty.

Respectfully,
Amira

Because the medical unit was giving me a hard time about going back to work and seeing the doctor from the medical unit, I decided to call my other union, Local-3. I told Ron what was going on, and I faxed him twenty-three pages, including letters from my doctor, all the light-duty forms that I had sent management, and the doctor from the medical unit.

SEPTEMBER 12, 2004

To Mr. Ron:
I want to file a grievance. I have been cleared to return to work by my doctor on light duty, immediately. Mr. Lawson and the medical unit are preventing me from seeing Dr. Perkins at the medical unit to be cleared to go back to work. I filed a grievance with my other union, Benjamin Abrams, President, about management and the medical unit preventing me from seeing Dr. Perkins. I want to go back to Tour-3; please help me.

Respectfully,
Amira

I wrote another letter to the postal medical doctor, and sent it certified mail.

SEPTEMBER 12, 2004
To Dr. Perkins, MD:
I am trying to return to work. My doctor cleared me for light duty, and management is preventing me from seeing you. I am seeking reemployment to go back to my Tour-3.

Respectfully,
Amira

I had gone one month without working, because Mr. Lawson was denying me the opportunity to return to work, so I decided to write him a letter.

SEPTEMBER 13, 2004

To Mr. Lawson:
I am still out, waiting to come back to work. I have bills to pay and responsibilities to meet, and without a paycheck I can't do it.

You have my current medical information, and are still not allowing me to come back to work. My doctor has requested that I return immediately. I am asking to be back on Tour-3, on a light-duty status. Several employees have been granted this accommodation. I feel that it is discrimination and retaliation for me coming forward about Mr. Lawrence.

I am still ready, able, and willing to come back to work on a lightduty status on Tour-3.

Respectfully,
Amira

September 16, 2004, the manager of attendance control sent me a letter stating that I was continuously absent without approved leave (AWOL) from duty, since August 26, 2004.

I wrote a letter to the MDO from Tour-1 on September 16, 2004.

To Ms. Lee:
The postal has kept me out of work. I'm willing and able to report back to work on Tour-3. My paperwork has been submitted, and I have been denied light duty.

Respectfully,
Amira

On September 18, 2004, I sent Benjamin Abrams, and Ron, the letter that I had sent to senior plant management, as well as my diagnosis from my physician.

On September 20, 2004, the congressman sent me a copy of the letter that the relations representative sent.

On September 21, 2004, no matter how many trips I took to my doctor's office to fill out all the forms that management was sent me, day after day; or how many times I went to talk to the union president at the job; or how much paperwork I sent to the medical unit, Dr. Perkins, management, and senior plant manager, I knew that I was wasting my time. What I did was call the Complaint Organization Department (COD), because this was another case.

Even with all the work limitation forms that my doctor had filled out and that I had sent to management, I could not return to work. So, I wrote a letter to the postmaster general on September 22, 2004, and sent it to him via express mail.

Dear Mr. Postmaster,

My name is Amira. I have worked for the post office for six years. The senior plant manager is Mr. Lawson. Mr. Osborne, I need your help; I have no one to turn to. I will make this as brief as possible. I have been sexually harassed from the year 2000 by my supervisor, Mr. Lawrence, and management has done nothing to solve the problem. I had a meeting with senior plant manager Mr. Lawson, my husband, and the president of the union, Benjamin Abrams. I worked on Tour-3 for five years. At the meeting, Mr. Lawson told me that he was not going to move Mr. Lawrence from Tour-3. Mr. Lawson gave me a choice: change to Tour-1, the midnight tour, or request a transfer to another station. Why? I am the victim. And I found out that Mr. Lawrence is sexually harassing another women. Why is management protecting him?

Mr. Postmaster, I have been out of work since August 13, 2004, from stress and other medical problems.

My doctor gave me permission to return immediately to work two weeks ago. I also requested to see Dr. Perkins from the medical unit to be cleared to go back to Tour-3 on a light-duty status.

Mr. Postmaster, I am still waiting to go back to work. I have bills to pay and responsibilities to meet, and without a paycheck, I can't do it. They have my medical information, and they still will not allow me to go back to work. Mr. Postmaster, by the way, they are prolonging my complaint.

Enclosed: Letter to Mr. Lawson - COD - Doctor's Letters

Respectfully,
Amira

The Complaint Organization Department (COD) sent me a letter dated September 22, 2004, for the petition I had filed against Mr. Lawrence.

On September 23, 2004, my friend from the job faxed me the petition list regarding the supervisor.

On September 24, 2004, I received a letter from the senior plant manager denying me light duty.

I called Benjamin and told him that I had received a letter from Plant Manager Mr. Lawson, denying my light duty; that I was still out of work, since August 13, 2004; and when I had left the job on that date, I didn't begin my tour. "It is not job-related." He told me to fax him the letter.

I sent the senior plant manager a second letter, stating that I had been out of work since August 13, 2004, and that I was ready, able, and willing to come back to work.

On August 26, 2004, I wrote a letter to the doctor from the medical unit:

My name is Amira. I was working on Tour-3. I made a complaint to management about a supervisor and his sexual harassment against me, and management changed me to Tour-1. Since they changed me to the night shift, my condition has become worse, and I am scared about my health. The night shift is killing me. I have been out of work since August 13, 2004. Dr. Perkins, please help me.

Sincerely,
Amira

Attached: Dr. Denson's letter and the medical information form that the RN from the medical unit sent me.

On September 27, 2004, I wrote another letter to the MDO from Tour-1 and sent it via certified mail.

To: Ms. Lee

This is to inform you that my paperwork from my primary doctor has been submitted to the senior plant manager and to the medical unit, to return back to work. I am willing to report back to work on lightduty status on any tour.

Respectfully,
Amira

After all those letters that I sent to the medical unit, and to the plant manager, they were still giving me a hard time about returning to duty. I wrote another letter to the medical unit doctor and sent it, via certified mail, to the medical unit office, with my diagnosis from my doctors and the worklimitation form.

SEPTEMBER 27, 2004

To Medical Unit Doctor:
This is the diagnosis you are asking for light-duty status, and the worklimitation form filed by my primary doctor. Please make me an appointment to seeyou as soon as possible.

Respectfully,
Amira

When I came back from the post office, I faxed Ron and Benjamin Abrams my FMLA papers and the notification of absence.

On September 28, 2004, I sent my supervisor, Mrs. Douglas, (Mr. Douglas's daughter) my FMLA papers, signed by my doctor, from September 27, 2004, with my 3972 Notification of Absence.

The plant manager was aware of my situation and my previous COD filing. Benjamin Abrams, my husband, and I had a sit-down in his office about this problem.

On October 5, 2004, l received a letter from Miss Wilson, a professional specialist. On October 13, 2004, I faxed Carol Barnes my FMLA papers and the certified mail receipt. On October 14, 2004, I received a certified letter from Ms. Lee.

On October 22, 2004, I wrote a letter in response to Ms. Lee, and sent it via certified mail.

SUBJECT: LIGHT DUTY

Ms. Lee,
Responding to your correspondence for my return to work on a lightduty status. Enclosed is a complete employee work-limitation form.

Respectfully,
Amira

When Don was calling for me to work, they were telling him that I didn't have any FMLA. Don called the Labor Board Agency, Hour Division, and told the woman who answered the phone that the problem I had at my job was with the FMLA. Anita Loos told Don that I had to write a statement from the day I left work. I wrote the letter, and I sent it to her, via fax, on November 2, 2004.

To: Labor Board Agency

On August 13, 2004, I, Amira, reported to work. My working hours are from 12:00 a.m. to 6:00 a.m. Before I began my tour, I felt very sick. I went immediately to report my illness to one of the MDOs who was in charge of the floor.
I told the MDO that I was sick and needed to go home as soon as possible. The MDO told me to fill out a 3971, which is a form to leave the job. I was unable to fill out the form, because I was very sick. The MDO said to me that she would fill it out for me, and that she would take care of it for me.
I left work to go to Queens. It takes about a one-hour drive to get back home. I made an appointment immediately to see my family doctor, Dr. Denson, who gave me a physical examination, stating that I was weak, with chest pains, and stressed, and that I was able to report to work immediately on a light-duty status.
The next step was to get in touch with the doctor from the medical unit, to be cleared. I spoke with the nurse in charge a number of times since August 13, 2004. I told the RN that I needed to make an appointment to see the

medical doctor, that it was an emergency, and that in order to go back to work, I needed to be cleared by the doctor. Mrs. Bette Davis, RN, stated that it was up to plant management.

Management and the medical staff are preventing me, up until the present time, from seeing the doctor. The postal policy is that, if you are out of work for a certain amount of time, you need to be cleared by your family doctor and by the doctor of the medical unit.

I sent all my medical information to the senior plant manager, the medical unit, and to other MDO person in charge of the floor. And I also stated that I was willing to work on any tour. There are three tours, and the post office has over 800,000 workers, and they are telling me that there is no work available for me, when there are many workers on a light-duty status. I've been working for the post office for six years.

On September 29, 2004, I filed an FMLA for a chronic, severe condition. I faxed it to Mrs. Carol Barnes. My husband also spoke with her on the phone. One month has gone by, and I have not received a phone call or any mail about my FMLA. I am waiting for a case number, and it doesn't take a month to qualify for FMLA. The post office is fully liable for this action.

I also filed a COD complaint a month ago about being cleared to go back to work. I have heard nothing from John Leland, who is in charge of the COD. I am willing and able to go back to work as soon as possible.

The post office has stopped me from making a living. I am falling behind on my bills and rent. Please investigate this matter deeply.

Respectfully,
Amira

On November 2, 2004, Carol Barnes sent me registered mail. On November 3, 2004, management sent me certified mail.

On November 4, 2004, I faxed some papers to Mrs. Loss, from the Labor Board Agency: *Mrs. Loss, this is the 3971 that I was talking about. This form was sent to me on September 14, 2004, from MDO Lee. I filled it out, with a request for FMLA leave, when I left work sick on August 13, 2004. Enclosed are my primary doctors letters*

On Wednesday, November 10, 2004, I faxed my Family and Medical Leave Act notice to Ron: *Ron this FMLA should cover me from August 13,*

2004, case number 1234567, up until November 13, 2004, which should be twelve weeks; I am also sending you the work limitation form.

The New York, Winston area sent me a letter on November 10, 2004, setting the date for my COD appointment for November 18, 2004.

On November 11, 2004, I faxed Ms. Loos, my FMLA officer, and I told her that it was the second FMLA that I had to fill out, case number 1234567.

And on Friday November 12, 2004, I sent Dr. Perkins my FMLA and my limitation form via certified mail.

On November 18, 2004, I received a letter from the Employee Standard Association, Office of Workers' Program and from DOPE Association, from the company's Injury Board Agency.

I faxed Ron the letters from my doctor.

On November 29, 2004, Mrs. Santiago from the postal service called me; she told me that I could return to work, and that I needed to write a letter to Senior Plant Manager Mr. Lawson, stating my request for light duty. I said to her, "Okay," but she said that I had to write a letter to him every month to request my light duty. I said okay. So I wrote him the letter.

Dear Mr. Lawson:
I am requesting light duty for thirty days.

Respectfully,
Amira/Tour-1

Four days after I spoke to Mrs. Santiago, I returned to work.

I faxed Ron the letters that Bette Davis and Dr. Perkins had sent me, dated November 26, 2004. But it was the same letter that Mrs. Davis, RN, had sent me on August 18, 2004. I also sent my doctor's letter from November 30, 2004, the work-limitation form from December 4, 2004, and the letter that I had received, dated November 30, 2004, from Carol Barnes, denying my FMLA.

On Monday December 20, 2004, Mrs. Santiago called me and told me that the senior plant manager took me off the clock. I asked her why I was taken off the clock, and she told me that it was because of a letter that my doctor had sent to the medical unit, stating that I couldn't work around machines. I told her that my doctor didn't write a letter stating that. She told me to call the medical unit, because she wasn't aware of what the letter stated. I called the medical unit to find out why Mr. Lawson had removed me from employment, a woman answered the telephone, and I told her my problem. She told me that I had to speak with Mrs. Bardot. And I left my telephone number with her, for Mrs. Bardot to call me.

On December 21, 2004, in the morning, when I was wearing a black silky nightgown, I received a call from Mrs. Davis's office for me to call Mrs. Jackie Collins for my qualification for light duty.

I called Mrs. Collins and I asked her why they had removed me from employment. She told me to hold on, and then she transferred the call to someone else. The person to whom she transferred me was Mr. Lawson, and I asked Mr. Lawson why he had taken me off the clock. He told me that my doctor had sent a letter to the medical unit stating that I could not work around machines. I told him that my doctor never gave me any letter stating that. I asked Mr. Lawson how I could get a copy of the letter that he was talking about. Mr. Lawson told me to talk to my doctor about it. I said to Mr. Lawson that I had the letters in front of me, and I didn't have a letter stating that I could not work around machines. I ended the conversation by saying, "Thank you."

When I hung up the telephone, I called Ron, and I told him about the conversation Mr. Lawson and I had just had. Ron told me to go to the facility and get the letter that my doctor had sent to management or the medical unit. I said, "Okay, bye."

I hung up the telephone, got dressed fast, got my car keys, and drove to my facility, walked straight to the union office, and spoke to Benjamin about Mr. Lawson taking me off the clock. Benjamin told me that he was going to ask for the letter, and for me to go home and call him as soon as I got there. After an hour of driving, I got home and called Benjamin. He told me that he had spoken with Mr. Lawson, who had told him that Dr. Perkins was the one who'd written the letter stating that I could not be around machines. On December 23, 2004, I received another letter from management, dated December 20, 2004.

I went to see my doctor on December 27, 2004, because I wasn't feeling well. I took the work-limitation form with me for him to fill out. The doctor advised me to stay home, because I was very weak. He gave me a note to go back to work on January 5, 2005. On the work-limitation form, he stated, "I sent the work limitation form to Senior Plant Manager Lawson."

On January 5, 2005, I went back to work after being out since August 13, 2004. When I reported to work, Ms. Lee told me to go to flat sorter 100 and talk to Mr. Parker, the supervisor in charge. Some of my friends from Tour-3 saw me going to the flat sorter machine and asked me how I was feeling. I told them I felt a little bit better, and, "Thank you." One of my friends told me to be careful, because Thomas was working as a supervisor on the flat sorter. I asked him which tour, and he told me Tour-3. He told me that he was still doing some paperwork on the computer, and for me to go the other way. Then he said to me, "Amira, good luck. We all missed you." I told him, "I missed all of you, too." And I thanked him and left to go to my working area.

I went to the flat sorter the way that my friend told me, but I saw Thomas. He just looked at me with a mean face, and I turned my head, looking for the supervisor who was in charge of flat sorter 100, to see which machine I was going to work on. I saw him and he told me to go to machine number seven. Every morning, when I went to my work area, I saw Thomas.

One night, some coworkers came to me and told me that Thomas was going to be transferred to another facility. When I heard that, I started to wonder why management didn't transfer Thomas when I had asked them to. The coworkers were telling me to come back to Tour-3. I told them no, because the damage was done, and going back to the tour would not bring my health back. Some of them got sad. I felt bad for them, because they wanted me back on the tour. But, like I always said, I had to do what I had to do. I had to find out why, when I asked for help in such an important situation, management turned their backs on me. It didn't matter how many letters I sent outside the post office, management from my facility didn't listen to my plea.

On January 10, 2005, I sent a certified letter to the senior plant manager, "Mr. Lawson," requesting light duty for thirty days, as well as the work-limitation form from my doctor.

Management sent me another work limitation form, and I took it to my doctor on January 21, 2005, for him to fill out.

A few days later, I sent the work limitation form, via certified mail, to Mr. Lawson.

On January 25, 2005, the medical unit doctor sent me another letter, with a work-limitation form to take to my doctor.

I took the letter and the work-limitation form to my primary doctor. He filled it out, and I sent it, certified mail, to the senior plant manager. On February 18, 2005, I took another work limitation form to my doctor, and he filled it out the same way that he did on January 25, 2005, and I sent it, certified mail, to Mr. Lawson.

Management sent me a response letter on February 28, 2005, dated February 24, 2005.

After reading management's letter, I went to see my doctor, because I was feeling sick, and I asked him for the letter of my diagnosis to be sent to management.

On March 1, 2005, I went to see my psychiatrist. She gave me a letter with my diagnosis to send to the plant manager.

On March 3, 2005, I went back to my doctor's office, because he had to fill out another work-limitation form.

On March 3, 2005, I sent the plant manager the letter from my psychiatrist and the work-limitation form that my doctor had filled out, together with the diagnosis letter and the letter requesting light duty for thirty days.

On March 28, 2005, I went to my supervisor, and I asked her to page my coworker friend, because I had left my reading glasses at home. She told me where I could find him, and she gave me permission to step off the work floor for a couple of minutes. I went to Harry's work area, and started calling him between the post-con. I saw him, and while I was walking an assistant supervisor, Julia Morley, coming from flat sorter 1,000 and started screaming at me, "Get out, get out!" I told her that I needed to talk to Harry, but she didn't let me talk. The only thing that she was saying to me, with a loud voice, was, "Get out, get out!" Then Julia turned to talk to Harry, and I waited there to ask my friend for his reading glasses. When Julia finished talking to Harry, she turned around and told me again to get out. I was trying to tell her the reason I was there, but she got very angry and assaulted me. She began to hit me and push me on the right side of my body, while screaming, "Get out, get out, get out!" I looked at Harry and gave him a shocked smile, and then she told me, "I am not kidding." Then she left. I asked Harry what was wrong with her, and he told me that she screamed at everyone. Then I asked him to lend me his reading glasses, and I left to go to my work area.

While I was working, I was thinking about what Julia had done to me, and I went to my supervisor, and told her everything. My supervisor told me that she was going to talk to MDO Jessica, because no one had the right to put their hands on me. I told her, "Okay."

My supervisor came back to me and told me that she had told Jessica what had happened, and then she told me that she was going to talk to Julia. She walked to flat sorter 1,000, where Julia was working, and minutes later she came back to me and told me that Julia had denied hitting me.

At about 5:25 a.m., my supervisor came to me to inform me that Jessica wanted to talk to me, and that I needed to go to the ATAL room. I went to the ATAL, and I told a supervisor who was there that Jessica wanted to talk to me, and she called her on the walkie-talkie.

Jessica came to the ATAL room, and we went into the management conference room. I told her everything that the assistant supervisor had said and done to me, and she told me that maybe it was because she had a lot of work. She told me that she was going to talk to Julia, because she had heard my statement, and she had to listen to hers. Jessica told me that she was going to get back to me. I told her, "Thank you," then I stood up from the chair, left the management conference room, and went to the cafeteria.

I got a cup of tea, and while paying for the tea I saw one of my friends, Jenny. I told her that Julia had hit me, and she told me that Julia had gone to flat sorter 100 and started screaming at her. She told me, "Amira, write her up," meaning I should make a complaint against her. I told her, "I can't believe what she has done to me."

When I finished talking to her, I sat down by myself, drank my tea, and at 6:00 a.m., I ended my tour and went home. I could not sleep. I was tossing and turning on the bed, thinking about what had happened to me at my job.

I called Benjamin, and I told him what had happened. He told me that he was going to report it, and he asked me if I had hit her back. I told him that I never could do something like that, and when I finished talking to him I went to my doctor, to take some papers for my work limitation.

While I was waiting at his office, my cellular phone rang. It was Don. He said, "Hey baby, how are you; where you at?" I told him I was at the doctor, and he asked me if I was okay, and I said to him, "Yeah I am fine," and he told me, "When you get home, we are going out to eat dinner," and I told him what had happened to me at the job. He could not believe it. He asked me if I had hit the assistant supervisor back, and I told him, "No, I did not hit her back." He told me that he would talk to me when I got home, and I told him, "Okay." I left the papers with the secretary, and I went home. When I got home, Don told me that he had called the inspector. I told him okay, and told him again what had happened, and I started crying and got very nervous. He told me that what the assistant supervisor did to me was very wrong, and that it should not be tolerated in the workplace. I told him I knew, but I couldn't understand why she had hit me. I told Don that I got very stiff and frozen.

On March 29, 2005, I had an appointment with my psychiatrist. I told her that an assistant supervisor had assaulted me, and she asked me if I had cried. I told her no, because I didn't want anyone to see my weaknesses. I asked my doctor for an update letter and she stated, *Please be advised that Mrs. Amira is still under my care with a diagnosis of adjustment disorder with anxiety.*

I finished my consultation, and while I was waiting for my next appointment, my cellular phone rang. When I answered, it was an inspector named Mrs. Nixon. She told me that my husband had called and left a message that I was assaulted on the job. I told her, "Yes, by an assistant supervisor." She asked me if I had told someone after it happened, and I told her that I had told my supervisor, and she had told the MDO. She asked me if I wanted management to take care of it, or if I want to make a complaint. I told her I wanted to make the report, because she could assault another person, or she could come back to me and assault me again. She told me to write a letter stating what had happened, put it in an envelope with the inspector's name on it, and drop it in the house box on the first floor.

I wrote a letter to the postal inspectors.

MARCH 29, 2005

To Postal Inspectors:

My name is Amira. I work as a mail processor on the flat sorter at the Winston Post Office. On Monday, March 28, 2005, at about 1:05 a.m. I asked my supervisor to page my friend to see if he could lend me his reading glasses, because I had left mine at home. My supervisor told me where he was working, and she gave me permission to step off the floor for a couple of minutes. I went to my friend's working area, and I started calling him between the post-con. I saw him, and a 204-B supervisor named Julia Morley was coming from flat sorter 1,000; the supervisor started screaming at me, "Get out, get out!" I told her that I needed to talk to Mr. Harry Vail, but she didn't let me talk. The only thing that she said to me was, "Get out, get out!" She turned to talk to Mr. Vail, and I waited there to ask my friend for his reading glasses, and when the 204-B supervisor finished talking to Mr. Vail, she turned around and told me again to get out. I was trying to tell her the reason I was there, but she got angry and assaulted me. She began to hit me and push me on the right side of my body, while screaming, "Get out, get out, get out!" Then she told me, "I am not kidding!" Then she left. I asked Mr. Vail what was wrong with her, and he told me that she screamed at everyone. Then I asked my friend to lend me his reading glasses, and I left to go to my work area. While I was working, I was thinking about what the 204-B supervisor had done to me, and I went to my supervisor and told her everything. My supervisor told me that she was going to talk to MDO Jessica, because no one has the right to lay their hands on me. I told her okay. The supervisor came back and went to talk to the 204-B supervisor. At about 5:25 a.m., my supervisor told me to go and talk to Ms. Jessica. I went to the management conference room, and I told the MDO everything that had happened. She told me that she was going to talk to her, and that she would have to get back to me.

I called Mr. Benjamin Abrams, the union president, and I told him what happened. He told me that he was going to report it.

Respectfully,
Amira

SEXUAL HARASSMENT IN THE POST OFFICE

One early morning, after 12:00 a.m., I was working, and my supervisor approached me to tell me that Jessica, whom I had made the complaint report to, wanted to talk to me. I went to the ATAL office, and there were Jessica and the shop steward who was going to represent the supervisor who had assaulted me. I asked for my representative, and the vice president came into the room and told me that she was going to represent me.

We went to the management conference room, and Jessica asked me to say what had happened on March 28, 2005, and told her to let Julia say what had happened first. The assistant supervisor started saying that she had told me that Harry was very busy, and he could not talk to me, and that I had started laughing, and that she had never assaulted me. Then Jessica asked me to say what had happened. I told them that, on March 28, 2005, I asked my supervisor to page my workmate because I had left my reading glasses at home, and she had told me where he was working, and she gave me permission to go and ask him for the reading glasses. When I got there, I started calling Harry. He looked from behind the postcon, and I walked to him. Julia came from flat sorter 1,000 and started screaming at me, telling me a couple of times to get. I walked to them, and I tried to tell her what I had gone there for, but she didn't want to listen to me. What she did do was turn around to talk to Harry, and I had waited there, and when she turned around and saw me standing there, she started to scream at me, and assault me, and began hitting me and pushing me on the right side of my body, while she screamed, "Get out." I told Jessica and the shop steward that I had looked at Harry and given him a shocked smile, and the assistant supervisor had told me that she wasn't kidding, and left. Jessica asked me what I wanted from her. Did I want a letter of apology? I told Jessica that I didn't need or want anything from that woman. And I asked her, "If I would have hit her on her lips and made her eat her teeth, would, I be sitting here right now?" She told me, "Thank you, Amira, for not responding." Then I asked Jessica, "Now can you tell me what you are going to do with her?" Her response to my question was, "What management is going to do is our concern." I told her, "Okay." Then Jessica told us that she had a written statement, and asked if we wanted her to read the statement, and if we wanted her to call in the person who had written it. I said, "Bring the person into the room." Then Jessica called for my witness. My friend came to the conference room. He sat down, and

Jessica asked him what had happened with the assistant supervisor and me. Harry told them that she had started to push me while she was telling me that I could not come inside where he was working. When I heard those words, I put my head on the table and said, "Thank you, thank you." Then Jessica told us that there would be an investigation.

On April 1, 2005, I took a work-limitation form to my doctor, and he also wrote me a letter.

I sent the letter that my psychiatrist and my doctor wrote to Mr. Lawson, via certified mail, with the work-limitation form and a letter stating that I was requesting light duty for thirty days

Management sent me a letter, dated April 9, 2005.

On April 11, 2005, My supervisor informed me that Cynthia Lee wanted to talk to me about what had happened on March 28, 2005, and that I should go to the ATAL office. I went to the office, and Ms. Lee told me that she had heard about what had happened to me, and for me to tell her, because she was on vacation, and that she had read the statement that my witness, Harry, wrote. I told Ms. Lee what the assistant supervisor did to me. She asked me, "In what position were you standing?" I showed her the same way that the assistant supervisor was hitting and pushing me. She told me that they were going to do an investigation, then she asked me how I was doing, and I told her, "Okay, thank you."

We finished talking, and I left the office. I was hoping that someone would care or take the matter of the assault seriously, but no one did.

When I got home, I took a shower and went to sleep, and when I woke up I called Ron and Oscar and told them what had happened to me at work.

On April 13, 2005, management sent me a letter, dated April 9, 2005, stating that my medical restrictions could not be reevaluated until my medical restrictions and physical limitations were properly evaluated by the postal medical officer.

After about two weeks, my friends came to me and told me that the punishment Julia Morley got was seven days' pay suspension. She said, "That's messed up." I said, "I know," and started walking to my working area.

On Thursday, May 5, 2005, at about 12:45 p.m., Mrs. Santiago called me to tell me that Senior Plant Manager Mr. Lawson had taken me off the clock, and that I was not to report to work. I asked Mrs. Santiago, "Why?" She told me that Mr. Lawson had denied my light duty because I could stand, bend, or twist for just one hour. I told her that I was going to look for my papers, but when I looked at the work-limitation form, there were three checkmarks. I told her that it was a mistake, because I could stand, bend, and twist. Mrs. Santiago told me to go to my doctor and fill out another work-limitation form. I asked her to fax me the form, because I didn't have one to take to my doctor, and she faxed me the form.

Friday May 6, 2005, I went to the office of my doctor to see if he could correct and replace the work-limitation form that he filed on April 29, 2005, and he corrected the error.

I went home and took a shower, and Don asked me if I wanted to go out to eat. I told him, "No, I don't feel good," and I went to bed. I woke up at 10:10 a.m., took a shower, got dressed, and got my purse, the paperwork, and the keys from my Jeep, and drove to work.

When I got to work, I went to the ATAL and left the form with Mrs. Clara, the secretary, to put in the MDO's mailbox. Then I went to the time clock and started to look for my badge to begin my tour at 12:00 a.m. but I could not find it, and I asked Mr. Parker why my badge wasn't on the rack. He told me to go to the ATAL and speak with Ms. Lee.

I walked to the ATAL, and I asked Mrs. Clara to page Ms. Lee, because she wanted to talk to me, and while I was talking to the receptionist, Ms. Lee came into the office and told me that she could not let me work. I asked her why, and she told me that it was Mr. Lawson's order. I told her that it was because of my limitation form, but I had gone to my doctor and he had corrected it. I told Ms. Lee that I gave the form to Mrs. Clara. She asked Mrs. Clara for the form, and Ms. Lee started to look at it. Then she told me to go to my work area, and that she was going to be there in a few minutes.

I went to my working area and waited for her for about ten minutes. While I was waiting for her, I started thinking that something was wrong, because if I was done talking to her, then why did I have to wait for her to start working? I looked for Mr. Parker, and I told him that I was waiting for Ms. Lee, and to please page her to see if I was going to stay at work or not. He called her on the telephone, and when he hung up the telephone he said to me, "Amira, sorry, I can't let you work tonight," and I said to him, "It's okay; bye, thank you," and I left the work area, went downstairs, got in my car, and while I was driving home thinking that these people thought this was a joke.

I pulled out a CD from Tego Calderon, put the CD player on, and started singing and listening to his song, "Los 12 Discipulos."

On Sunday, May 8, 2005, l called the presidents from the three unions: Benjamin, Ron, and Oscar. I told them that I had received a call from management on May 5, 2005, stating that Mr. Lawson had taken me off the clock, and for me not to report to work. They asked me why, and I told them about the work-limitation form. They told me to fax them the form that my doctor had filled out, along with the letter that the doctor from the medical unit had sent me. On the fax cover sheet, I wrote: *Sending you the work-limitation form from April 1, 2005. Mr. Lawson took me off the clock because, on the work-limitation form from April 29, 2005, my doctor stated that I could not bend, stand, or twist for more than one hour. It was a mistake, because when I went to see my doctor I told him that I was getting back pain, and he wrote that I couldn't bend, stand, or twist. So I went to my doctor on May 6, 2005, for him to correct the form, and management didn't let me clock in to begin my tour. I left the work-limitation form that my doctor had corrected with Ms. Lee, and I went home.*

On Monday, May 9, 2005, after I had gone to my doctor, I received a letter from the medical unit.

I received another letter on Saturday, May, 14, 2005, dated May 11, 2005.

On May 16, 2005, Don sent Mr. Whitehorn the letter that I sent to the postal inspector about the assault.

On May 19, 2005, I had an appointment with my psychiatrist. She asked me how I was doing, and I told her, "Not so good, because Mr. Lawson sent someone from management to tell me not to report to work." She asked me why he did that. I told her because of my work-limitation form. But I had gone to the doctor, and he had filled out another form, and I went back to work on Saturday, May 7, 2005, and management didn't let me work, and had sent me home. I was really sad when I told her. I wanted to cry, because reliving all those things that had been happening to me, which made me feel stressed out and weak after I finished talking about them.

SEXUAL HARASSMENT IN THE POST OFFICE

On May 21, 2005, I took another work-limitation form to my doctor. My doctor asked me, "What is it that these people want?" I told him that it was because they wanted to know how the myositis was diagnosed. My doctor filled out the form again, saying that I could lift more than forty-five pounds, and that with my left and right arms I could lift no more than thirty pounds each. My doctor circled all the other answers "Yes," and he stated, in letter "J," that I wasn't improving. And on top of the right side of the worklimitation form, he wrote that myositis was diagnosed with a physical exam. I sent all of my medical documentation by certified mail to Dr. Perkins, along with a letter:

Dear Doctor,

I am sending you the work-limitation form and the diagnoses that you requested, written on the same work-limitation form, as well as the letter of diagnosis from my psychiatrist.

Enclosed is a letter for Senior Plant Manager Mr. Lawson, requesting light duty for thirty days.

Respectfully,
Amira

On May 25, 2005, management sent me the same letter that I received on May 14, 2005. As soon as I read the letter, I called Mr. Adkins. He wasn't at his desk, and I left him a message, telling him about the letter for medical documentation and how, on May 23, 2005, I had sent Dr. Perkins all of the medical documentation that he'd requested. The next day, I received a call from Mrs. Santiago, and she had told me to hold on, because she was going to transfer me to talk to Mr. Adkins. I told Mrs. Santiago, "Okay."

When I was transferred to talk to him, I told him about the letter, and that I really didn't know what they wanted. He was on speakerphone, and Mr. Adkins asked me if I had gone to see Dr. Perkins. I told him that Mr. Lawson didn't want me to see Dr. Perkins. He told me to talk to the nurse from the medical unit, and I told him that the nurse, Mrs. Bette Davis, didn't want me to see the doctor, either. Mrs. Santiago, who was listening to the conversation, told me that she was going to transfer me to the medical unit office, that Mrs. Davis wasn't there, and to tell the other nurse about the paperwork I had submitted, because all the paperwork that I had submitted went to the medical unit and was confidential. I told her, "Okay."

Mrs. Santiago transferred me to the medical unit, and I told the nurse that I had submitted some paperwork to Dr. Perkins, and management was sending me a letter stating that the paperwork was insufficient. The nurse asked me when I had sent the documentation, and I told her that it was on May 23, 2005. She told me that she was going to look, and that she would call me back. The nurse called me and told me that my paperwork was on the desk, and as soon that they looked through the documentation that I had submitted, Mrs. Santiago would call me. I told her okay, and we ended the conversation. I started to think that, since August, 13, 2004, I'd been cleared by my primary doctor to go back to work, and I didn't understand why, from August 13 on, Dr. Perkins from the medical unit office had not spoken one word to me or even seen me to discuss my medical condition. If I was not mistaken, I thought, I should have been cleared by the medical doctor from the postal service, and I always asked myself why I was never checked out. I knew that I needed to see Dr. Perkins at his office, and he had to give me a physical exam to see if I was able to perform my work.

Now, I am still out of work, and I still don't know what management really wants. My life has changed since Thomas Lawrence sexually harassed me on my job, and management didn't want to believe me, and still don't believe me, saying that during the investigation there wasn't evidence that he was doing that to me. That is a lie. I have the proof. One of the managers came to me, assaulted me, screamed at me, hit and pushed me, but management didn't do anything about it. The only thing that they said was, "We will do an investigation." It was an investigation that benefited management, not the employees, because if an employee had assaulted a manager, that employee would have been fired immediately. And management has the nerve to talk about zero tolerance. What a line of shit that is.

www.ingramcontent.com/pod-product-compliance
Lightning Source LLC
Chambersburg PA
CBHW070723240426
43673CB00003B/127